MRCPsych Patient Management Problems Explained

Mo Zoha
Consultant Adult Psychiatrist
St Charles Hospital
Honorary Senior Lecturer
Imperial College
London

Jan Wise
Consultant Adult Psychiatrist
Park Royal Centre for Mental Health
Central Middlesex Hospital
Middlesex

Gary Wannan
Consultant Child & Adolescent Psychiatrist
Parkside Clinic
Notting Hill
London

John Lowe
Consultant Adult Psychiatrist
St Charles Hospital
London

D1438164

PASTEST
Dedicated to your success

© 2004 PasTest Ltd
Egerton Court
Parkgate Estate
Knutsford
Cheshire, WA16 8DX

Telephone: 01565 752000

First edition 2004

ISBN: 1 904627 021

A catalogue record for this book is available from the British Library.

The information contained within this book was obtained by the authors from reliable sources. However, while every effort has been made to ensure its accuracy, no responsibility for loss, damage or injury occasioned to any person acting or refraining from action as a result of information contained herein can be accepted by the publisher or the authors.

PasTest Revision Books and Intensive Courses

PasTest has been established in the field of postgraduate medical education since 1972, providing revision books and intensive study courses for doctors preparing for their professional examinations. Books and courses are available for the following specialties:

MRCP Part 1 and Part 2, MRCPCH Part 1 and Part 2, MRCOG, DRCOG, MRCGP, MRCPsych, DCH, FRCA, MRCS and PLAB.

For further details contact:

PasTest Ltd, Freepost, Knutsford, Cheshire, WA16 7BR
Tel: 01565 752000   Fax: 01565 650264
Email: enquiries@pastest.co.uk   Web site: www.pastest.co.uk

Cover design by Old Tin Dog Design Company
Typeset by Saxon Graphics Ltd, Derby
Printed by Page Bros. (Norwich Ltd)

CONTENTS

Contents

INTRODUCTION

Over the years many revision books have been written to help candidates pass the patient management problems (PMPs) section in the MRCPsych Part II Examination. In this book we have incorporated the best of the existing guides, as well as adopting an additional approach to help you improve your exam taking technique. We hope that this is a book that candidates will keep for further reference.

Each question in our book adheres to the exam format of a scenario and lead-in question, followed by supplementary information and additional questions. PMPs in the exam are designed to explore a candidate's ability to think on their feet and to elicit a solid and safe approach to everyday psychiatric problems.

We hope you will obtain useful information by reading through the model answers for each PMP. However the layout of this book has been deliberately designed for you to practise your PMP technique with others. To obtain the most from this book, we hope that you will gather together in at least pairs, with one adopting the role of examiner and the other as the candidate. This role-play should enhance your confidence and improve your preparation for the exam.

As the knowledge base of psychiatry advances, refinements and additions are needed to improve each answer. As each examiner will have his or her own idiosyncrasies when it comes to scoring candidates, we cannot provide a perfect response for any scenario. However the answer to each PMP in this book is comprehensive and up to date. Some of the questions may be at the boundaries of examinable topics and where included, this has been because of the importance of the area, the topicality of the subject or to provide a challenge to the more confident candidates.

We have included a "pointers and pitfalls" section at the end of each scenario to indicate how you could avoid failing that particular question, how you could extricate yourself from the rapidly approaching dead end of thought block or indeed how to excel in your responses. At the end of some scenarios, references have been included as a guide to further reading.

The "Gold Standard" answer to PMPs

To avoid unnecessary duplication, we have not included in every scenario advice on the standard approach to answering PMPs. We have therefore provided some general advice in this introduction.

The PMP candidate is expected to demonstrate the skills and knowledge developed beyond those of the part I candidate. So not only must you be able to demonstrate proper information gathering, appropriate investigations and a firm grasp of aetiology, but you must also indicate appropriate management and be sensitive to the wider issues of health service delivery.

Of course there is no such thing as a "gold standard" answer, but what follows is a systematic, thorough approach to any PMP. How much detail you go into and the points you decide to emphasise will depend on the subject of the PMP. Hopefully you will also have learnt from the examiners the most important areas on which to focus.

1 History and Examination

Many candidates wonder whether they should repeat the scenario to the examiners at the start of their answer. In our opinion, you never lose points for making sure you have grasped the essentials of the question. So when answering the first PMP of your exam, or subsequently if you find yourself at a loss, we would advise beginning by providing a précis of the salient features of the question, followed by the process of how one would complete an assessment. This might include the traditional "I would take a comprehensive history, perform a mental state, a physical examination and perform relevant investigations..."

The model answers in this book contain detailed information on aspects of the history and mental state you should focus on for that PMP. Where appropriate, comments on relevant aspects of the physical examination are included. Once this part of the assessment has been concluded, it is then necessary to move on to investigations. The most common investigations used by psychiatrists are now listed. The list is not meant to be exhaustive, with the answer to each PMP providing specific details on the use of relevant tests for that scenario.

2 Collateral information

One of the most important investigations performed by psychiatrists is the collateral history. Obvious sources of verbal information include the views of family members. However other people may have brought the person to your attention, such as the GP, ambulance drivers, police officers, or even a concerned neighbour. Each of these may hold valuable clues about the patient's mental health. It is important you pay particular attention to the information provided by the examiners about how the patient has presented.

Having exhausted verbal sources of information you should seek out written sources. It is worth asking if the hospital's discharge summaries, CPA (care programme approach) forms or clinic letters are available or accessible. Other sources may include social services notes, often kept separate unless case notes are fully integrated. Where there is a concern about the risk of harm to others posed by someone with a mental illness, the police have a statutory duty to disclose convictions to psychiatrists. Where further records are required, access to probation officer reports, educational reports and other medical records such as GP records or department of psychology records would be appropriate.

Where the patient has been admitted to a ward, obtaining reports of professional observations would be important. These would include those carried out by nursing staff, such as general behaviour, interactions with other patients, observations of sleep and dietary habits. Staff may also have been recording temperature, pulse and blood pressure charts.

There may be input from a psychologist, occupational therapist or a social worker. Their observations are likely to be important. Community psychiatric nurses may have knowledge of the family dynamics, the living circumstances, compliance with medication and may be able to advise on activities of daily living.

3 Further investigations

a) Blood tests

Relevant blood investigations may include haematological and biochemical indices. The widespread use of atypical anti-psychotics necessitates investigation of lipid profiles and fasting glucose levels. When harmful alcohol use or poor nutrition is suspected, obtain B12 and red cell folate levels. For IV drug users, exclude Hepatitis B and C infection. Obtain informed consent for HIV testing.

Testing for syphilis serology may be appropriate if a patient presents with features of neurosyphilis. If suspected, or the patient is taking medication such as lithium, endocrine abnor-malities including deranged thyroid hormone levels should be excluded. Other specific investigations which may be indicated include testing for specialised auto-antibody tests (eg when systemic lupus erythematosus is a differential) or the presence of poisons in the case of deliberate self harm or suspected organic conditions such as heavy metal poisoning.

b) Other bodily fluids

Properly supervised urine testing for the presence of illicit drugs can be a useful test for detecting substance misuse. In cases of acute confusion and pyrexia culture and sensitivity of urine, sputum, etc may be indicated. The presence of oligoclonal glands from cerebral spinal fluid is definitive in the diagnosis of multiple sclerosis.

c) Neuropsychological tests

These include those carried out by the psychiatrist themselves, such as cognitive state examinations. If more detailed testing is required, referral to a psychologist would be an appropriate investigation.

d) Electrophysiology

Electro-encephalographs (EEG) are useful for suspected epilep-tiform activity. Electrocardiographs (ECG) can exclude conduction defects such as prolonged QTc intervals when prescribed antipsychotics, or provide evidence of ischaemia in multi-infarct dementia.

e) Radiography

Radiography may include simple tests such as a chest X-ray, or more detailed computerised tomography or magnetic resonance imaging. The use of more complex scanning techniques such as MRI, magnetic resonance spectroscopy, or the radiation exposing single photon emitted computerised tomography or positron emission tomography are not yet widespread in psychiatry outside large research units. These tests could, however, be ordered if there are specific indications.

4   Diagnosis and Management

At the end of the assessment the candidate should have a preferred diagnosis, a list of differential diagnoses and be able to identify why the patient is presenting in this way at this time.

The construction of a coherent, systematic management plan is now possible. Management should address a combination of the patient's illness, their social conditions, their psychological motivation and any distracting or impeding factors such as marital or family relationships or conflict with the judiciary.

Management will need to be addressed on a biological, psychological and social level at the immediate, medium and long term. Consider all members of the multi-disciplinary team so that, for example, an intervention for treatment-resistant schizophrenia may include an antipsychotic, cognitive therapy, an analysis of carer needs and help with financial benefits.

A final note in preparation for the exams – cramming for 20 hours straight and taking concentration-promoting medication is unlikely to lead to success! A balance of planned work with appropriate breaks, nutrition and relaxation is the most likely path to success. Combining this with plenty of 'exposure' by practising PMPs with colleagues and educational supervisors should help reduce stress levels on the big day. We wish you all the best in your attempts to join the most exciting college.

Jan Wise and Mo Zoha

Scenario 1

A GP has referred to you a 28-year-old man. You are seeing him in a new outpatients clinic. The reason for referral is that the man is distressed as he has been hearing voices when no-one is around and is asking for help. How would you proceed?

Suggested Answers

- I would obtain a full history, perform a mental state examination and obtain relevant collateral information.

- In particular I would want to spend time addressing the presenting complaint and any relevant aetiological factors in detail.

Scenario 1 *continues*

In the course of your assessment you elicit information that the patient hears his father's voice calling out his name late at night, but does not hear voices at any other time. What other factors would you concentrate on in your assessment?

Suggested Answers

- I would want to clarify the nature of the patient's experience of hearing his father's voice. If the voice is only heard late at night, I would want to know if this was a hypnagogic hallucination. This would be the case if the voice was heard when the patient was drowsy and falling asleep.

- I would want to know what the significance of hearing his father's voice was to the patient, as this may be an important aetiological consideration.

- Other factors I would like to concentrate on are the presence of any other mental state abnormalities suggestive of mental illness.

Scenario 1 *continues*

You discover that his father died one year ago and eventually conclude that he is suffering from a pathological grief reaction. How would you help his distress? Is there a role for medication?

Suggested Answers

- I would want to explain to the patient the reasons for my formulation. I would explain the normal stages of grief and also the features of pathological grief.

- In order to ease his distress I would explain the nature of grieving, including that such hallucinations can occur as part of the normal grieving process. Depending on resources available to me, I would either refer the patient for bereavement counselling or I would perform this task myself. The aim of such counselling would be to help the patient come to terms with the death of his father.

- Medication can be relevant in grief reactions. Short-term use of benzodiazepines can be advocated in very distressed individuals in the early stages of grieving. Medication would also be indicated if an individual developed a depressive or psychotic episode.

Pointers/Pitfalls

- The best candidates are able to pick up on the direction in which the PMP is heading. Although examiners should not set out to trick candidates, almost all the information given will have some relevance and should not be ignored – in this case that the voice is of his father's.

- There are pros and cons of initially giving a 'standard type' answer by stating you would take a history, mental state examination and perform relevant investigations such as obtaining collateral information. One advantage of this approach is that you buy yourself a few seconds' thinking time to process the information given and then decide how to continue.

- PMPs often indicate a setting for your assessment and whether a patient is seeing you voluntarily. Be aware of this, but do not let this falsely assure you that there are no urgent problems and therefore neglect assessing risk.

- Management of a disorder should include an explanation of symptoms. This person has presented in a distressed state as he is hearing voices. Failure to explain the reason for hearing the voices would leave the patient still feeling distressed and would constitute inadequate management.

7

Scenario 2

You have been referred a 34-year-old man by his GP. The referral letter describes symptoms consistent with a diagnosis of depression. The reason for referral is that the GP has been unable to help alleviate his patient's complaints of depression and is asking for advice. How would you proceed?

Suggested Answers

- I have been described a GP referral of a patient whose symptoms of depression have not improved with the GP's intervention(s).

- I would proceed by performing a full assessment of the patient's symptoms, history, mental state examination and obtaining collateral history from the GP including treatment interventions attempted so far.

- I would want to establish the diagnosis of a depressive episode, its aetiology, its severity and consider any other relevant factors from my assessment.

Scenario 2 *continues*

The GP informs you that three different antidepressants were prescribed, but there was no improvement with any of them. The patient confirms he tried the three different preparations. How would you proceed?

Suggested Answers

- I would want to establish a number of facts. These include whether the patient had an adequate therapeutic trial of each medication. What were the patient's or GP's reasons for stopping medication? If adequate trials of antidepressants were undertaken, is this a case of treatment resistance?

- Therefore, to clarify these issues I would ask about the length of treatment with each preparation, whether the dose was increased to the maximum or whether there were any significant side-effects that led the patient to stop taking treatment.

Scenario 2 *continues*

The patient states he tried each antidepressant at the starting dose for a few days only. He states he does not like taking tablets and is asking if there are any alternatives to medication for depression. In particular he asks about cognitive behavioural therapy (CBT) for depression, as he has read about this in a magazine. How would you respond?

Suggested Answers

- Initially I would want to ascertain the level of the patient's knowledge of CBT and if necessary correct any misconceptions.

- I would then explain that CBT is an accepted and available treatment for mild to moderate depressive episodes. I would explain that CBT can be effective as an alternative to antidepressants, although I would add that CBT in conjunction with medication may confer further benefits.

- Finally I would explain the nature of CBT and how it could be specifically useful to this patient. I would do this by using examples of the patient's depressive cognitions I had elicited from my assessment. For example, if the patient over-generalises by drawing negative conclusions about himself based on one event, I would explain this to the patient. If the patient was able to make some sense of this explanation, he would be likely to benefit from CBT. I would therefore refer him for CBT or perform this treatment myself.

Pointers/Pitfalls

- The initial answer to this PMP uses an alternative way of using a 'standard' answer. This method incorporates repeating back aloud the salient features of the PMP. The advantage of this method is that it buys a few seconds' thinking time, as well as providing the examiners an opportunity to assess your ability to accurately précis and prioritise information given to you.

- When a patient has been referred by another professional with an attached diagnosis – in this case depression – you must still make it clear you would clarify the diagnosis yourself by performing an appropriate assessment.

Scenario 3

You have been asked to see a 28-year-old woman who complains of being preoccupied with food to such an extent that she can no longer cope with her daily living. How would you proceed?

Suggested Answers

- I have been described a 28-year-old lady with symptoms of a potential eating disorder. However, the presenting complaint could be part of the psychopathology of a number of disorders.

- I would therefore perform a full assessment, paying particular attention to the presenting complaint of preoccupation with food.

- I would try to establish whether the patient has an eating disorder. If so, are there any associated physical complications that need urgent management, for example severe electrolyte disturbances secondary to recurrent self-induced vomiting?

- Being aware that eating disorders can often present with additional symptoms, I would establish whether there any other disorders present such as depression, or maladaptive patterns of coping such as substance misuse.

Scenario 3 *continues*

After your assessment you conclude that the patient fulfils the criteria for bulimia nervosa. How would you manage this patient?

Suggested Answers

- I would explain to the patient what I thought was the nature of her difficulties and discuss what potential treatments were available. I would then proceed to explain my management plan to the patient.

- I would decide on what setting the patient would need to be treated in. Depending on the severity of her presentation, it is most likely that I would treat her as an outpatient or day patient. I would also decide on referral to a specialist eating disorders unit if that resource was available to me.

- I would undertake any appropriate short-term interventions (for example, correction of electrolyte imbalance).

- As a day patient or outpatient I would perform a further psychological evaluation, followed by a cognitive behavioural approach if appropriate. CBT should aim to address concerns prominent amongst patients with bulimia nervosa, such as self-image, attitudes to weight and body image, impulse control, maladaptive coping mechanisms, etc as well as any underlying depressive symptoms.

- Some evidence exists to advocate the use of antidepressants both for depressive symptoms and also for poor impulse control and I would consider whether it would be appropriate to undertake a trial of an antidepressant.

Pointers/Pitfalls

- Be particularly aware of mental disorders that may have serious complications for the physical health of a patient. In the case of bulimia nervosa, mention that you would want to exclude the possibility of risks such as electrolyte imbalance or abuse of laxatives or insulin. Make it clear to the examiner that you are aware of such complications and that you would assess and manage these appropriately.

- Most PMPs will assume you do not have access to specialist services such as an eating disorders clinic. You may mention that you would refer appropriate patients to such facilities, but you would be expected to describe in detail the management patients would receive were they to be treated in such units.

Scenario 4

You are asked to see a 56-year-old man in clinic. He has admitted to his GP that he has problems with alcohol and wants to cut down his intake. How would you assess this man?

Suggested Answers

- I have been described a middle-aged man who has been referred by his GP for alcohol-related problems. I would therefore want to perform a full assessment, paying particular attention to the man's alcohol history.

- I would want to establish the amount of alcohol the man consumes by adding his weekly consumption of units. I would also assess the pattern of his consumption. I would also want to investigate the presence of any other mental disorders and assess whether any previous attempts have been made to address the alcohol problem.

- In addition to taking a full history and performing a mental state examination, I would carry out a physical examination, looking in particular for evidence of neurological or liver damage.

- I would also perform appropriate laboratory tests as indicated from my assessment. These may include a full blood count, mean cell volume (MCV) and biochemistry including liver function tests.

- From my assessment I would want to ascertain whether his use of alcohol is either harmful or dependent. In particular I would want to assess the degree of any psychological or physical complications from his alcohol use. I would determine whether the patient has alcohol dependence syndrome by looking for the following features:

  ○ Stereotyped pattern of alcohol use.

  ○ Primacy of drink-seeking behaviour.

  ○ Compulsion to drink.

  ○ Withdrawal symptoms.

  ○ Relief drinking to avoid withdrawal symptoms.

  ○ Tolerance to alcohol.

  ○ Reinstatement of previous pattern of drinking after a period of abstinence.

Scenario 4 *continues*

Your assessment concludes that the man has alcohol dependence syndrome, but that he has had a successful home detoxification through the GP the previous week. The man is asking if he can return to controlled drinking rather than abstinence. How would you advise him?

Suggested Answers

- I would initially discuss the alcohol dependence syndrome in appropriate detail so that any decision the patient makes is an informed one. I would explain the high risk of reinstatement after abstinence. This would make the strategy of controlled drinking a high-risk one, as it may rapidly lead to a dependent pattern of consumption.

- Having discussed the nature of the syndrome, I would then spend time discussing the patient's options with regard to management. As the patient has alcohol dependence syndrome and therefore established psychological/physical complications from his use of alcohol, I would explain the benefits of maintaining a period of abstinence. This would aid the patient by allowing a period of recovery for his physical problems. It would also permit the patient to fully engage in appropriate psychological management to help him with his alcohol dependence.

- Psychological management could include the patient's attending 12-step meetings such as those organised by Alcoholics Anonymous. Alternatives include receiving cognitive behavioural therapy, with emphasis on strategies such as relapse prevention.

- I would consider the role of medication. As a detoxification has already been undertaken by the GP, there should be no need for benzodiazepines. Depending on the patient's neurological status and diet, it may be appropriate to prescribe thiamine for a period of time. Acamprosate may also be useful if cravings are a prominent feature of the patient's dependency.

- Finally I am aware that patients with alcohol dependence often have adverse social situations as a result of the primacy of their alcohol usage. I would therefore consider the need for any social interventions, depending on the result of my assessment of the patient's social situation.

Pointers/Pitfalls

- The use of terminology, such as 'primacy' or 'reinstatement after abstinence' demonstrates your expertise in a subject to the examiner. Therefore, when delivering your answer to a PMP consider the appropriate use of such terms, rather than a description of the term.

Scenario 5

You have been referred a 36-year-old man by his GP. The referrer states that the patient has had obsessive compulsive disorder for over ten years. This has been untreated as he has refused to see a psychiatrist or accept help from his GP. The patient is now agreeing to see a psychiatrist and you are reviewing him for the first time in clinic. How would you proceed?

Suggested Answers

- I would perform a full assessment by obtaining relevant collateral information, taking a full history and performing a mental state examination.

- In particular I would want to assess which symptoms are most distressing for the patient, as well as establish why the patient has now agreed to a psychiatric review.

Scenario 5 *continues*

The patient describes repeated thoughts that he must stop consuming all food and water. As these thoughts are becoming more intense and harder to resist, he has reluctantly agreed to seek medical help.

Suggested Answers

- Having elicited distressing and potentially life-threatening symp-tomatology, I would want to establish the diagnosis. I would determine whether the patient's thoughts are obsessional in nature – as the GP has suggested – and whether there was a depressive or psychotic component present.

- Having established the diagnosis, I would want to clarify and address any relevant aetiological factors. In particular I would want to determine the reason for the exacerbation in his symptomatology.

Scenario 5 *continues*

You establish that the patient has obsessive compulsive disorder with no prominent features of any other mental disorder. How would you manage his distress?

Suggested Answers

- In the short term I would assess the seriousness of the risk, in particular that to the patient's health. I would want to exclude the possibility that the patient has stopped eating and drinking as a result of his obsessional thoughts.

- If he had, is he dehydrated and in need of urgent medical attention? I would want to assess whether the patient was willing to undergo treatment for his obsessive compulsive disorder. If the risk was immediate, I would consider the need for using the Mental Health Act.

- If the patient is still eating and drinking, I would identify and address any potential precipitating factors that would result in his stopping eating and drinking.

- With regard to the more long-term management of the patient, I would consider whether there is a role for medication. Given the reluctance to seeking medical care, I would assess whether there is any resistance to taking psychotropic medication. If so, I would try to explain the potential benefits of a trial of medication. In particular I would explain that an antidepressant such as clomipramine or a selective serotonin reuptake inhibitor may help reduce his symptoms.

- I would also discuss potential psychological treatments for obsessive compulsive disorder, including CBT (cognitive behavioural therapy). I would explain the rationale for CBT and that it is more likely to be effective when used in conjunction with medication.

Pointers/Pitfalls

- The management of most psychiatric conditions will involve medication, specific or supportive psychological interventions and possible social interventions. To impress your examiner, tailor your answer to incorporate the specifics of the content of the PMP.

- Therefore in this PMP, highlight the fact that this patient has been unwell for ten years but did not seek medical attention. This suggests a recent change which needs investigating, as well as a possible underlying reluctance to see a psychiatrist or accept psychotropic medication. These factors will of course affect management of the patient's condition.

Scenario 6

The mother of a 24-year-old female patient of yours wants to see you to discuss her daughter's illness. How would you proceed?

Suggested Answers

- Initially I would need to establish with the patient whether she gives consent for me to discuss her illness with her mother, or any other named relative, carer or friend.

- If the patient refuses I would explore the patient's reasons for not wanting me to discuss her illness with her mother and if appropriate try to reassure the patient as to the nature of any discussion.

- I would be aware of the mother's right to be involved in her daughter's care – particularly if she is the principal carer. I am also aware that the mother may wish to disclose important collateral information which would not require me to disclose confidential information about the patient.

- If the patient does consent, I would ask whether the patient wishes to be present at all times when discussions are held with her mother, or if she is happy for me to see her mother alone. Finally I would clarify with the patient whether there is anything she specifically does not want mentioned or discussed with her mother.

Scenario 6 *continues*

The patient gives consent for you to discuss her illness with her mother and does not want to be present in the meeting. The patient has recently been diagnosed with schizophrenia during this first contact with mental health services. In your meeting, the mother would like to know whether her daughter's condition is permanent. How would you advise her?

Suggested Answers

- I would initially establish how much the mother already knows with regard to her daughter's diagnosis. I would also establish the extent of her knowledge regarding schizophrenia and address any specific fears or queries that she has.

- I would then provide the mother with information about schizophrenia, its course and its treatment. I would provide the mother with information regarding schizophrenia associations, including ones aimed at relatives and carers of individuals with schizophrenia.

- To answer the mother's query about whether her daughter's condition is permanent, I would relate the patient's prognosis to her individual characteristics. Although it is essential to be truthful, it is helpful to try to maintain a positive outlook rather than induce a negative frame of thinking.

Scenario 6 *continues*

The patient's history is that she lives with her mother and five siblings in a three-bedroomed house. She became unwell after losing her job and then taking a binge of stimulants over the following weekend. She started becoming increasingly aggressive and perplexed until, after an urgent visit, she was admitted informally. She was unwell for six weeks after admission with prominent first-rank symptoms. She subsequently responded to a trial of an atypical antipsychotic. How would you advise patient and mother with regard to prognosis?

Suggested Answers

- I would advise mother and patient that although prognosis cannot be precise, there are a number of good prognostic factors present. These include clear precipitants to the illness in the form of job loss and substance misuse.

- I would also advise that prognosis can be influenced by a number of factors such as adherence to therapy. Hopefully the atypical antipsychotic which led to recovery is acceptable by the patient for prolonged usage.

- Another factor that would need investigation is the patient's social environment. I would want to exclude the presence of high expressed emotion as an aetiological factor. If present, I would want to start family therapy combined with psychoeducation.

Pointers/Pitfalls

- The first part of this PMP involves the issue of consent. It is important to demonstrate to the examiners that you are aware of the legal issues regarding consent. However, you should also be aware of the rights of carers, in this case the patient's mother.

Scenario 7

A solicitor has asked you to see a local patient in order to prepare a medical report. The purpose of the report is to support his appeal against a Home Office decision to refuse him asylum. You agree to see the patient and arrange for an interpreter to help with translation. At interview the patient states he was persecuted in his home country as he belonged to a religious minority. How would you continue with the assessment?

Suggested Answers

- I would complete a thorough assessment by taking a history and performing a mental state examination, focusing on the following factors:

  o In view of the presenting complaint, I would particularly want to ask about the nature of persecution and whether there have been any long-term psychological consequences as a result.

  o I would be aware that it may be especially important to obtain a cultural perspective by obtaining collateral information regarding the patient from any friends or relatives.

  o A physical examination may be important, particularly if the patient alleges he was tortured and as a result has suffered permanent physical handicap or scarring.

Scenario 7 *continues*

The patient tells you that he was arrested, interrogated and repeatedly tortured over a six-month period. His family eventually managed to bribe corrupt prison officials, who then organised for the patient to escape. The patient then fled the country and entered the UK illegally, claiming asylum. The solicitor believes his client has 'PTSD' (post-traumatic stress disorder). How would you confirm this and what associated psychopathology would you particularly assess for?

Suggested Answers

- To establish the presence of PTSD I would determine whether the key features of PTSD were present. These would be the presence of:
  - ○ Onset of symptoms within six months of a severely traumatic event.
  - ○ Persistent re-living of the trauma in the form of flashbacks or nightmares.
  - ○ Avoidance of stimuli which would remind the patient of the trauma.
  - ○ Any additional features such as hypervigilance and autonomic disturbance.

- I would assess for evidence of any co-existing mental illness such as depression or anxiety, or less common problems such as psychosis.

- I would also assess for evidence of maladaptive coping strategies such as substance misuse.

Scenario 7 *continues*

You conclude that the patient does have PTSD with associated depressive features. How would you manage this case?

Suggested Answers

- The patient has been referred by a solicitor for a legal report. The patient has features of mental illness, namely PTSD and depression. It would therefore be appropriate to offer the patient help. I would need to decide whether it was appropriate for me to also provide psychiatric care for the patient, as this was not the original intention of the referral.

- On the assumption that I take on the management of this patient, I would consider appropriate pharmacological, psychological and social interventions.

- In view of the depressive symptomatology, a trial of an antidepressant would be indicated.

- Psychological therapy would also be indicated. Cognitive behavioural therapy has been shown to be effective for patients with PTSD, however the patient's lack of English may present a barrier to efficacy.

- I would therefore enquire about any voluntary organisations – such as the Medical Foundation for Victims of Torture – that may exist locally. Such organisations may be able to provide psychological help in the patient's own language.

- Refugee support services also often exist where there are large concentrations of refugees and may be able to provide help with further psychological support and practical advice.

Pointers/Pitfalls

- Be aware of the role of voluntary organisations and mention them if appropriate. These organisations are valuable resources and by mentioning them to your examiner, this demonstrates your awareness of the role of non-statutory bodies to provide help for sufferers of mental illness.

- Any PMP where an interpreter is mentioned as being part of the assessment may need a number of factors addressing. These include the accuracy of interpreting and disclosure of confidential information which may be too sensitive to reveal via a relative. For this reason it is preferable to use a professional interpreter. In cases such as this one, you may need to be sensitive that the interpreter may belong to an opposing religious or cultural group – this could have significance with regard to whether the patient is prepared to be open.

Scenario 8

You have been referred a 72-year-old man and plan to assess him in clinic. He has been diagnosed with Parkinson's disease and has been treated successfully for two years initially by a neurologist and then his GP. The GP has referred the patient as he has started to develop intrusive auditory hallucinations. How would you proceed?

Suggested Answers

- I would perform a full assessment of the patient by taking a history, examining his mental state and performing a physical examination, paying particular attention to his neurological system.

- As part of my assessment I would determine whether the patient has a past history of psychotic symptoms, or whether these are new symptoms.

- It would also be important to determine whether the patient is in receipt of any medication which may be affecting central dopamine levels. If so, these could be contributing to the aetiology of the hallucinations.

- I would also assess whether there are any other likely precipitants for the hallucinations, such as stressful life events, co-existing mental illness or substance misuse.

Scenario 8 *continues*

You do not elicit any other significant aetiological factors other than the onset and treatment of Parkinson's disease. You conclude that the patient's parkinsonian symptoms have been well controlled since starting 'levodopa'. However, he does have second-person auditory hallucinations that are very distressing. How would you manage this patient?

Suggested Answers

- I would explain to the patient that a possible cause of his hallucinations is the treatment he is receiving for his Parkinson's disease.

- In order to treat the hallucinations, I would explain that it may be necessary to reduce his levodopa. Hopefully this would still provide adequate treatment for his Parkinson's, whilst extinguishing his hallucinations.

- Any decision I would make to reduce the treatment for his Parkinson's disease would involve consultation with the patient's GP or the neurologist.

Scenario 8 *continues*

The patient agrees to a reduction in his medication, but his hallucinations persist. How would you then treat him?

Suggested Answers

- It would then be appropriate for a trial of an antipsychotic. It would be important to select an antipsychotic with a low propensity to produce parkinsonian side-effects. Therefore, it would be preferable to use an antipsychotic with limited dopaminergic activity, such as quetiapine or olanzapine.

Pointers/Pitfalls

- For patients with co-existing physical disease it is important to mention that you would involve other relevant medical staff in important decisions that might affect these conditions. In this case the GP should be involved. If treatment suggested by you compromises the patient's physical presentation, it may be appropriate to re-refer to the neurologist.

Scenario 9

You are called urgently to attend a ward where you find a young female patient who is struggling whilst undergoing a physical restraint by two male nursing staff. How would you respond?

Suggested Answers

- I would make a quick initial assessment of whether or not the restraint appeared to be properly controlled. Given that the patient is continuing to struggle, that she is female and the staff all male, and that a restraint would not usually be attempted with fewer than four to five nursing staff, I would have a high index of suspicion that the restraint was not adequately or appropriately controlled.

- If so, I would ensure that the senior nurse in charge had been contacted in order to request that an adequate number and gender mix of nursing staff be summoned. Only if I was trained in restraint, and whilst awaiting the arrival of extra staff, might I offer to assist with the restraint itself.

- Otherwise I would remain physically present in the vicinity of the restraint and might attempt verbally to calm the patient.

Scenario 9 *continues*

Extra members of staff arrive, including two female members of staff, and controlled restraint is achieved. However, for the moment the patient remains physically restive and verbally abusive. What would you do next?

Suggested Answers

- I would take a history from the member of staff with the best knowledge of the patient, preferably away from the patient.

- I would also want to inspect the patient's clinical notes and drug chart.

Scenario 9 *continues*

After ten minutes staff find that they are able to relax and terminate the restraint. A female member of staff takes the patient to her room. What would you do next?

Suggested Answers

- I would take the opportunity to review the patient's clinical notes and drug chart, and liaise with staff more fully.

- I would then interview and examine the patient, including a mental state and physical examination.

- I would ensure that I was supported and appropriately chaperoned at all times by nursing staff.

- If at all unsure I would seek the advice and support of more senior medical staff.

- I would take appropriate action depending on my assessment, eg offer oral sedation.

- I would document my assessment and actions in the medical notes.

Pointers/Pitfalls

- The key here is not to rush prematurely into action, eg rapid tranquillisation. Your first duty is, as far as possible, to ensure the safety of the patient, your colleagues and yourself. Having done so you can then set about making an assessment in order to determine the nature and cause/s of the disturbance that led to the restraint, eg akathisia due to neuroleptics or uncontrolled psychotic symptoms, etc. Appropriate treatment can then be prescribed. It is also vital to remember that the patient may have suffered adverse consequences – physical and/or psychological – as a result of the restraint and that these will require medical management in their own right.

Scenario 10

At an outpatient Care Programme Approach Clinic, the partner of a 35-year-old male patient with a diagnosis of schizophrenia reports increasing disturbance due to relapsing auditory hallucinations. The partner asks that the patient's current medication be changed; she has heard that a 'new' drug called 'Clozapine' is the 'answer' to the problem. Before making your decision, how would you respond to the partner's request?

Suggested Answers

- I would explain to the patient and his partner the licensed conditions for the use of clozapine in terms of the potential benefits and risks. Based on this information I would check the patient's preference and their capacity to give informed consent.

- I would assess whether the patient met conditions for a trial of clozapine. Namely, has the patient failed an adequate therapeutic trial of at least two different antipsychotics?

- I would consider whether the partner's report of relapsing symptoms was accurate or whether this was a way of expressing some other kind of difficulty arising in their relationship.

- If there did indeed appear to be a relapse of symptoms I would try to determine whether the primary reason was due to emerging pharmacological resistance, or whether some other factor was more likely to be responsible, eg inadequate dosage, intolerance, poor compliance, substance use, social stressors, co-morbidity, etc.

- Finally, I would check that there were no absolute contraindications, eg a history of myocarditis or agranulocytosis, and take into account any relative contraindications, eg diabetes or ischaemic heart disease.

Scenario 10 *continues*

You determine that the patient is a suitable consenting candidate for clozapine, although you note a strong family history of ischaemic heart disease. How would you proceed towards the introduction of clozapine?

Suggested Answers

- I would provide the patient and partner with verbal and written information in a suitable form. I would discuss the case with my Consultant and multidisciplinary team.

- I would register myself (the prescriber), the patient and the supplying pharmacist with the Clozaril Monitoring Service.

- I would take baseline physical measures, including bloods (full blood count, liver function tests, thyroid function tests, fasting lipids and blood glucose), blood pressure, pulse, temperature, ECG and weight.

- I would consider which method of drug substitution would be most suitable, eg cross tailing.

- I would also consider whether hospital admission is necessary or whether continued close monitoring could be conducted in the community during the period of titration.

Scenario 10 *continues*

The patient is established on clozapine and the partner reports a good response; however, six months later she expresses the concern that the patient seems more breathless than before after climbing the stairs to their first floor flat. How would you manage this problem?

Suggested Answers

- I would suspect an underlying adverse reaction; in particular, weight gain, myocarditis, ischaemic heart disease or anaemia.

- In particular I would:
  - Carry out a physical examination and take a history.
  - Re-check the patient's weight.
  - Re-check other physical indices, including blood pressure, pulse, temperature, bloods, blood glucose and ECG.
  - Liaise with the GP.

- If their weight had substantially increased, I would refer the patient to a dietician.

- If other indices were deranged, I would refer the patient to a Specialist for advice, and review the risk assessment.

- I would consider stopping the drug and making an urgent medical referral if the patient's physical health appeared to be rapidly deteriorating.

Pointers/Pitfalls

- It is important not to neglect reasons other than emergent pharmacological resistance that might explain the reported symptomatic relapse. Monitoring of the metabolic and cardiovascular as well as haematological risks associated with clozapine is essential.

Scenario 11

An 18-year-old man with a first episode of psychosis, probably schizophrenia, is admitted to an acute psychiatric ward. Staff report that during visits he and his mother quarrel furiously and subsequently the patient becomes aggressive and appears more disturbed by psychotic phenomena. Otherwise he appears to be making good clinical progress in response to treatment. How would you assess this situation? What causes would you consider?

Suggested Answers

- I would review the relational history between the patient and his mother. I would discuss the case with other staff and look at the notes.

- In particular, I would interview the patient and seek his permission to discuss his case with his mother.

- I would assess the carer's needs and difficulties and find out whether she understands her son's illness. I would also need to know if she has a mental health problem herself, eg schizophrenia, and if she is emotionally dependent on her son.

- I would consider obtaining a third party history, eg from the other parent or a sibling, after first obtaining consent to do so from the patient.

- I would interview the mother and son separately, and together.

- I would exclude substance supply and use as a cause, and consider requesting a urine drug screen.

Scenario 11 *continues*

Your inquiries reveal a history of a close but conflictual relationship, with hostility and criticism observed between mother and patient at interview. Father seems rather cold and marginal. The mother appears to be particularly intolerant of her son's lingering delusional suspicions about the food that she brings him each evening. Drug use is not thought to be a factor. What is the 'diagnosis' or problem? How should it be managed on the ward?

Suggested Answers

- I would conclude that the 'diagnosis' or problem is high expressed emotion.

- I would suggest the following ways to manage the situation on the ward:

  - I would try to limit face to face contact between the patient and his mother, clearly explaining my reasoning for doing so.

  - I would then suggest that any contact between the two be supervised.

  - Depending on resources available to me, I would either refer the patient and his mother for psycho-education or I would perform this task myself.

  - I would refer the patient to CBT/family therapy if this resource were available.

Scenario 11 *continues*

Following your intervention the mother's level of hostility is seen to diminish along with the patient's distress and disturbance, during and after visits. The patient continues to make good progress and is nearing discharge. He intends to return home to his parents. How might support for the mother be extended into the community?

Suggested Answers

- I would want to extend support for the mother into the community by preparing a pre-discharge meeting under the Care Programme Approach (CPA).

- I would make sure that the patient and his mother were able to continue with the CBT and the Family Therapy.

- I would allocate a Care Co-ordinator.

- I would carry out a Full Carer's Assessment, including carer's strengths and weakness; for example, financial, physical, mental and social aspects.

- Where there are identified weaknesses I would consider intervening; for example, making sure that the patient and his mother were claiming all appropriate State Benefits, and giving them information for referral to carers' support groups, eg Mind.

- I would refer the patient to a day centre or occupational programme to limit excessive contact at home.

Pointers/Pitfalls

- This question gives the candidate an opportunity to demonstrate that they appreciate the social aspects of the management of mental illness, specifically schizophrenia. To do this it is helpful to think about the patient and the illness in relation to the wider social system.

- A good candidate will show that they can consider how the key elements in the social system interact to affect the course of the patient's illness. For example, mother has a poor relationship with her partner, and therefore is emotionally dependent on her son and less able to tolerate his symptomatic suspiciousness, leading to conflict, thereby aggravating his symptoms, and further marginalising the father, and so on.

Scenario 12

An 18-year-old young woman presents to A&E in a distressed state seeking medical help for a reported overdose of 30 paracetamol tablets. The patient is seen first by the Casualty Officer who refers her to you because she has refused a blood test. How would you respond to this referral?

Suggested Answers

- I would briefly check to see if the patient is previously known to A&E and/or psychiatric services.

- I would then try to find a quiet private area suitably chaperoned.

- In particular I would start by taking a focused history and assessing her mental state. I would check the details of, and circumstances surrounding, the overdose.

- I would attempt to understand the motivation for the patient's refusal to accept treatment, eg whether she is paranoid, depressed or has needle phobia.

- I would make a risk assessment.

- I would make an initial assessment of the patient's capacity, ie a one-doctor assessment.

Scenario 12 *continues*

It transpires that the patient took an impulsive overdose following an argument with her boyfriend. He confirms that she took 30 tablets of paracetamol approximately two hours ago. The patient is quite clear that she doesn't want to die, but hates needles and just wants to go home and make up with her partner. There are no signs of a depressive or psychotic illness. She says that once when her GP offered her a tetanus vaccination she fainted and that since then she has been 'terrified of needles'. What is the likely diagnosis? How would you categorise the risk? What would you do next?

Suggested Answers

- Given this information, I would make a diagnosis of a stress-related impulsive act whose treatment is complicated by needle phobia.

- I would consider that she is a potentially high-risk patient.

- I would then explain to the patient why further assessment and treatment is necessary and that this will require venepuncture. I would discuss ways in which the experience might be made more bearable, eg by sedation, local anaesthetic, emotional support.

Scenario 12 *continues*

The patient then begins sobbing and keeps insisting that she just wants to go home. Do you allow the patient to return home? If not, under what powers would you detain them and with what purpose? What is capacity? How should it be assessed?

Suggested Answers

- I would not allow the patient to return home.

- I would use the Common Law – Doctrine of Emergency – in order to detain this patient and treat her by force if necessary.

- In order to be considered competent – ie having capacity – the patient should be able to understand and believe, retain and weigh in the balance the essential information you provide regarding the nature of the problem and the need for treatment. NB There is a high threshold for high-risk situations.

- Capacity should be assessed by at least two doctors. In such situations it would probably be wise to consult with senior colleagues, namely the A&E and Psychiatric Consultants.

Pointers/Pitfalls

- Clearly, the most important point to grasp here is that this is a potentially life-threatening situation. Urgent medical intervention is required to prevent serious harm. Although the patient is technically an adult, given her youth, situation, distressed state, phobic condition, and in particular her stated wish not to die, it would seem primae facie that the balance of her mind is disturbed to a degree that she is unable to make an adequately informed and reasoned decision about the need for treatment. Arguably the Mental Health Act (MHA) could be applied – for the treatment or prevention of a physical problem arising out of a psychiatric condition, namely needle phobia. However, in practice, the delay involved would rule this out as the option of first choice.

Scenario 13

You are called urgently to a ward where you find a 29-year-old male patient under a controlled physical restraint. The nurse in charge explains that the restraint has been in progress for 15 minutes with little or no sign of the patient settling or accepting oral medication. You are asked to consider prescribing rapid tranquillisation. How would you proceed?

Suggested Answers

- I would start by making a quick assessment to establish the likely cause of the disturbance.

- I would liaise with the nurse in charge.

- I would then attempt to take a brief history from the patient, and perform a mental state examination.

- I would then review the patient's medical notes and drug chart, taking particular note of recent medications and any intolerance to them.

Scenario 13 *continues*

Your assessment reveals that the most likely cause of the acute disturbance is substance use leading to an exacerbation of psychotic symptoms associated with aggression towards others. The patient is in receipt of a conventional depot neuroleptic. You elect to initiate rapid tranquillisation. Which drug or drugs would you prefer, at what dose and how would you administer the drug/s?

Suggested Answers

- To initiate rapid tranquillisation, I would prefer a drug that has a rapid onset of action with minimal side-effects; therefore, my rational first choice would be a short-acting intramuscular benzodiazepine such as lorazepam 2 mg.

- Given that the patient is already receiving a conventional depot neuroleptic, I would carry out rapid tranquillisation with a neuroleptic such as haloperidol 5 mg more cautiously because of the risk of acute dystonia. However, this would depend on the dose of the depot and the history of sensitivity.

- I would avoid giving the drug intravenously because of the risk of cardio-respiratory arrest. I would determine the dose by referring to clinical factors such as the patient's drug history, level of disturbance and weight.

- I would ensure that basic life support equipment and the benzodiazepine antidote flumazenil were available on the ward before administering the tranquilliser.

Scenario 13 *continues*

Following an intramuscular injection of lorazepam 2 mg the restraint is successfully terminated and the patient escorted to his bed to 'sleep it off'. What further management would you undertake?

Suggested Answers

- I would carry out a full physical and mental examination of the patient as soon as practicable following their restraint.

- Following their rapid tranquillisation, I would ensure that the patient was closely observed by nursing staff over the next two to four hours.

- In particular I would want to have their vital signs, eg blood pressure, pulse, temperature and oxygen saturation (if available), monitored at regular intervals, say half hourly.

Pointers/Pitfalls

- It is vital to make an assessment, however provisional, of the nature and causes of the disturbance. As far as possible individual patient factors and susceptibilities should be taken into account when prescribing. Once sedation is achieved it is important to provide post-restraint support and monitoring.

Scenario 14

A 45-year-old man with schizophrenia and a deteriorating mental state is referred by a concerned GP. In particular the patient complains that he can feel an octopus in his stomach, which he is threatening to cut out himself unless it is surgically removed. How would you want to assess this patient's complaint?

Suggested Answers

- I would want to make an urgent assessment of this patient with schizophrenia and deteriorating mental state.

- In particular, I would take a full history and perform a mental state examination as well as a physical examination to exclude an acute abdomen. This would include a full blood count, urea and electrolytes, liver function tests and an abdominal x-ray.

- I would want to obtain collateral information, by liaising with the patient's GP.

- I would want to review the patient's notes, in particular looking at his treatment, risks and aetiological factors.

- I would consider arranging to make a home visit with the Community Psychiatric Nurse and GP.

- I would consider making an assessment under the Mental Health Act if the patient declines further.

Scenario 14 *continues*

A review of the case file reveals that the patient is well known to the service and that he recently commenced clozapine to good therapeutic effect. The Clozaril Patient Monitoring Service reports that the patient has been attending regularly for blood tests and that poor compliance is not suspected. The complaint of an 'octopus' in the stomach is new. On examination the patient's abdomen is distended but non-tender. The patient has not had a bowel motion for three days but is passing flatus. The abdominal x-ray shows distended loops of large bowel. Bloods are normal. What is the likely diagnosis? What treatment should be prescribed?

Suggested Answers

- I consider that the likely diagnosis is constipation secondary to clozapine (because of its anti-cholinergic action). I would also consider the possibility of paralytic ileus and keep the patient under review.

- I would seek the advice and support of the pharmacist and other more senior medical colleagues.

- I would start treatment with laxatives, eg lactulose ± senna, fluids and soft diet to relieve the constipation.

- I would monitor the patient, in particular their abdomen, bowel function and vital signs.

- I would try to prevent this from happening again; in particular I would encourage the patient to change his diet to include more roughage and more fluids. I would also consider reducing his clozapine dose.

- I would consider admitting the patient to hospital or increase his support in the community in order to administer his treatment, monitor progress and maintain safety.

Scenario 14 *continues*

The patient responds well to treatment and subsequently attends a routine outpatient appointment. His psychiatric symptoms appear well controlled on clozapine maintenance. How might you work to maintain and improve the patient's physical health for the future?

Suggested Answers

- To maintain and improve the patient's physical health for the future, I would work jointly with the GP both in and out of Clinic, with the primary care liaison nurses and link workers.

- In particular, I would want to implement a physical screening programme, including weight/BMI, blood lipids, blood pressure, blood glucose, dental hygiene, chest function (namely, peak flow measurements) and ECG. This would entail referring him to other specialists, for example a dentist.

- I would back this up by giving the patient advice about a healthy lifestyle, including the importance of diet, not smoking, taking exercise and avoiding substance misuse.

Pointers/Pitfalls

- It is important to recognise a potentially life-threatening situation and respond in a timely and proportionate fashion.

- Remember that a deterioration in mental state may be due to a reaction to underlying physical disease particularly if the symptoms, however bizarre, point in that direction.

- Potentially life-threatening ADRs (adverse drug reactions), however rare, eg paralytic ileus, should always be borne in mind and explicitly excluded in your answer.

Scenario 15

A 28-year-old man with schizophrenia who is apparently relapsing attends A&E with his mother requesting a prescription. Mother is keen to look after the patient at home. The patient is said to have a history of violence when unwell. You have been asked to undertake a risk assessment. How would you proceed?

Suggested Answers

- Considering that the patient has a history of violence when unwell, my first priority would be to ensure a safe setting for his assessment.

- In particular I would want to ensure the safety of the patient, his carer, other staff and myself. Therefore, I would alert Security to the possibility of an incident and insist that another member of staff was present throughout the interview, which I would arrange to be conducted in a suitably safe setting.

- I would liaise with Casualty staff and any other available professional informants; I would also review his notes.

- I would determine the level of risk for assessment.

- When all preparations are complete, I would conduct a thorough clinical interview with the patient. In particular, I would observe the interaction between him and his mother. I would also seek consent from the patient to interview his mother on her own.

- I would discuss risks and treatment options frankly but sensitively with the patient and his mother.

- I would identify important actuarial (eg past history) and clinical (eg mental state) factors, and formulate these to arrive at a risk categorisation – a hypothetical statement including the impact, likelihood, confidence and time span of a given risk for a particular set of conditions. The precise format will probably be determined by local procedures.

Scenario 15 *continues*

Assessment reveals from the old notes that there is a history of acute relapse characterised by delusions, thought disorder and hostility, associated with non-compliance and substance misuse leading to compulsory admission. In the last five years there have been a total of two episodes of violence occurring against fellow in-patients resulting in minor injury. There are no issues of treatment intolerance or resistance. On examination the patient is irritable but not overtly threatening; although suspicious, he is rational and coherent. Insight seems to be good. Mother and son demonstrate a sound relationship and, when taken aside – with the ready agreement of the patient – the mother confirms a recent history of poor compliance with medication, and that she is willing to care for her son including ensuring compliance. She adds that she has not attempted to do this before but feels that on this occasion the relapse has been 'caught early', and that therefore she is willing to try. Mother and son both independently deny recent drug use. Casualty Staff confirm that the patient has been 'no problem' whilst in the Department. There is nothing to indicate risk of harm to the self.

Following this formulation how would you categorise the risk? What further information or investigations might you seek? What further management would you undertake?

- Given this information I would be reasonably confident that the short-term likelihood of serious harm to others is low should the patient go home with his mother, plus a prescription and enhanced community support. Arguably, the risks might be greater were the patient to be admitted.

- If available, I would refer the patient and his mother to the local home treatment or crisis resolution team.

- I would ask for a urine drug screen and arrange liaison with the Community Mental Health Team (CMHT), as this would be helpful in both clarifying and potentially minimising the risks to the patient and his mother.

Scenario 15 *continues*

All the indications appear to be favourable and the patient is discharged. However, he re-presents two weeks later in a deteriorated state. Mother says that although the patient has been taking the tablets she has not been able to dissuade him from the heavy use of cannabis. She feels she cannot cope with her son's escalating and unprecedented delusional threats of physical violence towards her, and she is seeking admission for him. The patient wants to be allowed to return to his mother's home. He denies substance use. A urine drug screen is positive for cannabis. In the light of these developments you are asked to review the risks. What is your revised assessment? What action would you recommend?

Suggested Answers

- This new information indicates to me that the clinical risks appear to have increased considerably.

- In particular, there is the new and potentially serious risk of the patient suffering from unprecedented delusions of a violent nature towards his mother. Also, there is evidence that he is using cannabis, although he denies it. I now feel that treatment at home is unlikely to prevent a progression of the patient's illness.

- I would recommend admitting this patient, if necessary using the Mental Health Act. I would recommend this because of the patient's deteriorating condition at home and his mother's request that he be admitted because she no longer feels able to cope and is in danger. As part of my new risk assessment, I would review the patient's level of security of placement.

Pointers/Pitfalls

- The basis of a good risk assessment is a good psychiatric assessment.

- Ensure your own safety.

- Gather as much relevant information as is practicable, in order to make a preliminary assessment of risk before you see the patient.

Scenario 16

A GP has referred to the local Learning Disability Team a 45-year-old man with Down's syndrome who lives in low-support hostel accommodation. There is a two-month history of 'out of character' angry outbursts directed towards other residents, whom the patient accuses of interfering with his possessions. There is no past history of mental illness and the patient's learning disability is thought to be in the mild to moderate range. The patient is a smoker but otherwise the medical history is unremarkable. As the psychiatrist with the Learning Disability Team you are asked to make an assessment. How would you proceed? Indicate the diagnoses you would seek to exclude.

Suggested Answers

- I would obtain a full history, perform a mental state examination and obtain relevant collateral information.

- In particular, I would liaise with the GP and hostel where the patient is living, and where the 'out-of-character' outbursts have been taking place.

- I would give careful consideration to the conditions under which assessment should take place, paying particular attention to when and where it should happen and who else should be present.

- I would prepare by examining any old records to establish the patient's pre-morbid baseline, including any psychometric estimates of his IQ.

- I would also want to clarify the history of the presenting case; in particular I would want to find out details of the patient's behaviour, any precipitants to the 'outbursts', the consequences of his actions, his relationships with other hostel residents and details of any recent life events. I would then consider whether his pattern of behaviour is 'understandable' given his situation, and if his situation is 'abusive' in any way.

- I would then obtain a functional history, looking in particular for any evidence of decline prior to his presentation. I would consider whether the pattern of any decline is suggestive of a particular diagnosis or diagnostic group.

- I would carry out a Mini Mental State Examination (MMSE).

- I would apply suitable caution when applying any diagnostic tools, making sure that they have been standardised appropriately. In particular, I would be aware that the MMSE may be subject to 'floor effects' and therefore lack the required precision.

118

- I would also carry out a full physical examination, obtaining the patient's temperature, pulse and blood pressure. I would examine the cardiovascular system looking in particular for signs of ischaemic heart disease.

- I would request special investigations as well, including thyroid function tests, a full blood count, ECG, EEG, IQ and infection screen as indicated.

Use this page to write notes

Scenario 16 *continues*

Hostel Staff tell you that, in spite of being an incorrigible chain smoker, the patient was previously well settled for many years. However, over the last 18 months there has been mounting difficulty with the performance of certain tasks such as managing money and running errands, which are best characterised as 'forgetfulness'.

On one memorable occasion the patient wandered the streets all night apparently because he was 'lost'. The angry outbursts seem to be in relation to accusation of theft concerning possessions, eg sweets, which subsequently 'turn up' apparently where the patient himself had left them.

The mental state examination reveals an overweight amiable character in possession of basic verbal communication faculties, and a MMSE of 5, but is otherwise not noteworthy. Baseline psychometry was not available. Physical examination demonstrates a raised blood pressure of 170/100mmHg and a carotid bruit. Bloods including thyroid function tests are normal.

What is the most likely diagnosis? What would be the management?

Suggested Answers

- Given the patient's smoking history and his presentation I would make a diagnosis of vascular or multi-infarct dementia.

- I would refer his cardiovascular management to a cardiologist for specialist investigation and treatment, including an ECG, treatment with anti-hypertensives and aspirin, as well as giving dietary and lifestyle advice.

- I would continue his psychiatric management, working with the patient and the hostel staff to contain his behaviour using psycho-educational and supportive environmental measures.

Scenario 16 *continues*

Following treatment with aspirin and atenolol the patient's cognitive decline is substantially slowed, if not arrested. However, it was felt that the increased care needs merited a transfer to higher supported accommodation. Following this the patient has become withdrawn, tearful and irritable. When approached by staff all he will say is 'I'm dead'. How would you formulate this new situation? What would be your management?

Suggested Answers

- I would want to review the patient and re-examine him.

- I would diagnose the patient to have probable depression or an adjustment reaction secondary to his move and/or his anti-hypertensive treatment.

- I would consider using social, psychological and pharmacological interventions to manage his depression, the choice being determined by his illness severity, his preference and capacities and local service factors.

- I would also discuss alternative anti-hypertensives with his cardiologist.

Pointers/Pitfalls

- Be sure to demonstrate that you are aware of the specific implications of learning disability/Downs in terms of the practicalities of assessment, the precision of certain diagnostic procedures and the range of diagnostic possibilities.

- However, don't get too narrowly focused too soon – the opening scenario is deliberately ambiguous and your management approach should reflect this, ie cast a wide net.

- Do always seek to establish a baseline.

- Don't forget about physical conditions and the physical examination.

- Don't be shy of saying that you would refer to other medical specialists where this seems appropriate, but do convey at least an undergraduate knowledge of what the outcome of such a referral might entail in terms of further management.

Scenario 17

A colleague confides in you that they are experiencing trouble in their training. How do you proceed?

Suggested Answers

- I would firstly make sure that there was adequate time to explore the topic, and that there was privacy.

- I would clarify what the 'trouble' is; in particular, I would want to find out whether the trouble is related to the trainer, team, colleagues, syllabus or something else.

- I would want to establish whether the problem is interpersonal, organisational, intrapersonal, psychological or financial.

- In particular, I would want to know whether it is bullying or harassment, related to race, gender, religion or sexual orientation.

Scenario 17 *continues*

After further exploration the colleague tells you that she is concerned about her supervision. How would you look into this further?

Suggested Answers

- I would want to find out whether my colleague is receiving regular (weekly) face-to-face meetings with her consultant in which the focus is on the trainee's needs, and not just a review of the case load.

- To establish the level and nature of her supervision, I would concentrate in particular on whether:

  ○ The log book is being used in a systematic manner.

  ○ The material being covered is suitable to her training requirements; for example, if she is about to sit an exam, are the sessions more exam focused?

  ○ She is determining the agenda in collaboration with her Consultant.

  ○ She is deciding what her needs are.

  ○ She is concerned about the Consultant's knowledge or skills. Or his behaviour.

- I would also want to find out whether her non-clinical needs are being ignored, such as pastoral care or personal matters, eg dependent children/partner/parent.

Scenario 17 *continues*

After further questioning you notice a lack of initiative in your colleague. You were a previous trainee of her Consultant and found her Consultant to be supportive and stimulating. You suspect your colleague may have burn out. What is burn out and how can one avoid it?

Suggested Answers

- Burn out syndrome was first described by H Freudenburger in 1974.

- Its main features are:

  o Emotional exhaustion.

  o Depersonalisation.

  o Low personal accomplishment.

- Burn out syndrome is associated with anxiety, depression, sleep problems and functional somatic complaints of the cardiovascular and gastrointestinal system.

- Primary causes of burn out syndrome are:

  o High demand in conjunction with low influence.

  o High level of engagement with insufficient reward.

  o Low level of social support.

  o Maladaptive cognitions, especially those involving unrealistic levels of control; and perfection.

- One can avoid burn out syndrome by taking the following preventive measures:

  o Balint-style groups.

  o Psychotherapy/alternate cognitive styles.

  o Supportive supervision.

- A useful reference about burn out syndrome is:

  Schaufel, W, Maslach, C, Marek, G. 1993. Professional burnout: recent developments in research and theory. Florence K, Taylor and Francis.

Pointers/Pitfalls

- This scenario could easily expand to consider depression in the trainee; or a personal, medical or professional issue with the trainer. If the latter were the case candidates would be best advised to diplomatically approach, or advise approaching the relevant senior manager.

Scenario 18

Occupational Health have asked you to see a 31-year-old female psychiatrist with a history of bipolar affective disorder and a serious suicide attempt. She is due to begin a new post with the Trust. How do you proceed?

Suggested Answers

- First I would obtain all relevant medical records, including contacting her GP and prior treating Consultants, and I would obtain her discharge summaries.

- Then I would arrange to see the patient after clarifying with Occupational Health what their concerns are. In particular I would want to know why I am being asked to see her and why the treating psychiatrist is not being asked to provide a report.

Scenario 18 *continues*

Occupational Health wish to know if you agree that the patient has a disability and whether any additional support is required. After interviewing the patient you decide that she is currently stable. She is not currently seeing a psychiatrist. How do you proceed?

Suggested Answers

- I would divide the concerns into two areas: the first relates to clinical questions and the provision of care to the patient; the second addresses organisational issues.

- Regarding the clinical questions and provision of patient care, I would want to establish:
  ○ Her risk of relapse, even though she is stable at the moment.
  ○ Whether she is compliant with her medication.
  ○ Her current and predictable stressors.
  ○ Her support networks, socially, academically and clinically.

- Regarding the organisational issues, I would want to establish:
  ○ Why she is not registered with a GP. Failing to be registered may have relevance to the health section of appraisal as well as being against General Medical Council guidelines.
  ○ Whether she has a fear of stigma.
  ○ Whether there is a disagreement over treatment, or concerns over confidentiality. The patient needs to be registered with a psychiatrist, if possible one with expertise in treating doctors.
  ○ Whether the tutor/scheme organiser has been made aware, so that appropriate pastoral support and monitoring can occur. I would be aware that whilst employers have a duty to make reasonable adjustments to the post so that the patient can perform her duties, there is also a duty to protect patients.

Scenario 18 *continues*

You discover that the situation is rather different to your first impression. She is depressed, having given birth four months previously. Following an argument there is little parental support. She stopped her SSRI and mood stabiliser during her pregnancy and is currently breast-feeding. How do you proceed?

Suggested Answers

- This new information, that the patient recently had a baby, means that I have had to reassess the situation. In particular, I have a duty of care towards the patient whilst safeguarding the interests of her child.

- For the patient, I would enquire whether she has suicidal thoughts or abnormal beliefs about the baby.

- I would need to find out how severe the depression is.

- I would also want to determine whether the patient should be at work and, if not, for how long she should stay away.

- I would want to explore how to improve her support networks.

- I would also want to find out why there was an argument with her parents. It would be important to be aware of any cultural values at stake and whether this row means the removal of a significant source of support. I would look into the possibility of mediation.

- I would determine whether a Community Psychiatric Nurse is required to monitor the patient or provide support.

- It would be important to find out how involved/aware the partner is, and whether their needs have been assessed.

- I would follow recommendations that, on becoming pregnant, patients with a history of serious mental illness are re-graded to receive enhanced status on the Care Programme Approach.

- With regards to medication I would discuss the risks of remaining depressed and the benefits of treatment.

- I would attempt to discern the patient's perceived negatives of medication. Appraising the patient of findings about SSRI use during breast-feeding, namely that there is negligible secretion, may lead to acceptance. Likewise discussion of the risks of mood stabilisers such as valproate and carbamazepine may improve concordance.

- Finally, I would want to safeguard the interests of the child. In particular, I would want to make sure that there was a separate assessment of the child's requirements.

- I would want to decide if and when child protection services should be informed.

- I would need to be confident that the process of care review has been 'protection proofed'. I would be aware that it is fairly easy to overprotect the mother, whom services may erroneously treat as a special case due to the medical connection, whilst not looking after her and her child's interests equally. It is a valid point that the service is an advocate of the patient. However, there is a statutory duty to consider the child's welfare.

Pointers/Pitfalls

- The GMC take a very dim view of doctors treating themselves or their family for any but the mildest conditions. If self-treatment is occurring then further action may be necessary; potentially ending in a report to the GMC's health section.

- As may be seen from the references provided this is a very recent issue. It is a prime example of a critical question where there is little tolerance for an inadequate response.

- References:

  Report of an Independent Inquiry into the Care and Treatment of Daksha Emson MBBS, MRCPsych, MSc and her Daughter Freya. London: North East London Strategic Health Authority, 2003.

  Hendrick, V. *et al.* 2001. Use of sertraline, paroxetine and fluvoxamine by nursing women. *British Journal of Psychiatry*, 179, 163–6.

  Epperson, C.N., Jatlow, P.I., Czarkowski, K., Anderson, M.A. 2003. Maternal fluoxetine treatment in the postpartum period: effects on platelet serotonin and plasma drug levels in breastfeeding mother-infant pairs. *Pediatrics*, 112 (5), e425–9.

  Carers Recognition and Services Act 1995.

  The Victoria Climbie Inquiry – Report of an Inquiry by Lord Laming. London: Department of Health, 2003.

Scenario 19

You are a Consultant. A new patient, a 68-year-old male, was admitted by your Senior House Officer last night. His relatives had brought him up saying he was a little odd and having difficulty at work. Nursing staff report that he is slightly inappropriate and wet his bed that morning. When he comes into the ward round you note that he seems to have a slight stagger. How would you proceed?

Suggested Answers

- I would obtain a full history and check the results of the physical examination, perform a mental state examination and obtain relevant collateral information.

Scenario 19 *continues*

It appears that at work he is failing in duties he was previously competent at. There are complaints of lethargy, easy fatigability and vague weakness of the legs. For six months his family have noted that he is dull and forgetful.

Further exploration for symptoms of depression reveals no other possible somatic or cognitive symptoms.

Cognitive state examination reveals some mild impairment of registration and recall but little else. At the physical state examination upgoing plantars were found with no other unequivocal signs.

What further action should be taken?

Suggested Answers

- I would request a battery of blood tests for:

  ○ Potentially reversible causes of dementia.

  ○ Renal function.

  ○ Hepatic function.

  ○ Haematinics.

  ○ B_{12}/folate levels.

- I would be suspicious of normal pressure hydrocephalus, because of the signs of urinary incontinence, poor memory and gait abnormalities. The remaining steps I would take would be to confirm the diagnosis with a cranial CT and intracranial pressure monitoring.

Scenario 19 *continues*

What is the prognosis? What may other cerebral investigations show?

Suggested Answers

- I would reassure the patient that, if treated, his prognosis for a substantial recovery from normal pressure hydrocephalus is excellent:

  ○ A recovery of over 40 IQ points has been reported after eight months of symptoms (McHugh, P.R.).

  ○ Similarly, many of the neurological signs can resolve.

- I would arrange for EEG monitoring, which may show theta and delta waves but is often normal.

- I would also request a CT, as this is the investigation of choice for detecting changes in ventricular volumes.

- A CT would reveal whether there were any space-occupying lesions, which are another cause of hydrocephalus as they obstruct the drainage of cerebrospinal fluid. Headache is often a complaint.

Pointers/Pitfalls

- It is acceptable for a candidate to fail to identify the condition but in that case they must identify that the gait abnormality and incontinence are pathological and an urgent referral for a neurological opinion is required. The saving feature of this response is that the candidate is clearly identifying an abnormality and the limits of their knowledge; a failure to practise within one's limits being a recipe for contact with the General Medical Council in the future!

- Reference:

  McHugh, P.R. 1966. Hydrocephalic dementia. *Bulletin of the New York Academy of Medicine*, 42, 907–17.

Scenario 20

A 58-year-old male became forgetful and disoriented at Christmas. This was attributed to heavy alcohol consumption and depression. His marital situation and business affairs had deteriorated. When admitted to hospital six months later his mental state showed marked variability with disorientation and memory disturbances fluctuating with periods of lucidity. He was emotionally labile and gave approximate answers. How would you manage the situation?

Suggested Answers

- I would manage this situation by obtaining a full history, performing a mental state examination and obtaining relevant collateral information.

- In particular, I would want to obtain a 'dementia screen'.

Scenario 20 *continues*

You find out that in March he had a fractured neck of femur, and underwent hip replacement surgery. Neurological examination reveals a pout reflex and shuffling gait, but little else. Blood investigations reveal no abnormalities. He is apyrexial with nothing cultured from cerebrospinal fluid (CSF), no white blood cells in the CSF and no increased glucose. The dementia screen reveals nothing. How do you proceed?

Suggested Answers

- I would consider whether the deterioration could have been caused by a fat embolus following the fractured neck of femur; however, the time course rules this out.

- I would recommend that further observation on the ward of the patient is warranted.

- I would want to make further investigations, in particular an EEG and CT/MRI are appropriate.

Scenario 20 *continues*

The EEG shows prominent slow waves, maximal over the left fronto-temporal region. The MRI shows generalised atrophy. His speech becomes incoherent, he is doubly incoherent and he has gross apraxia with myoclonic jerks. Choreo-athetoid movements develop. What are your concerns and how would you manage the situation?

Suggested Answers

- I would be concerned that the patient clearly has a rapidly progressive dementia, with no identifiable cause from non-invasive tests. I would be suspicious that Creutzfeldt–Jacob disease (CJD), or bovine spongiform encephalitis are possibilities. In this case I would manage the situation symptomatically, my aim being to help the family. I might order a repeat EEG at this stage, which may show triphasic discharges.

- In particular, I would be concerned about the typically rapid progression of the clinical features of CJD and variant CJD (vCJD). I would be sure to explain this in detail and with care to the patient's family and I would look for signs of fatigue, insomnia, anxiety and depression with gradual changes to slowness and unpredictable behaviour, as these are prodromes of the disease. Occasionally the mood is elevated with inappropriate laughter. I would be aware that sometimes cognitive deficits or neurological signs develop later on and that this can mislead one to suspect a functional disorder.

- I would expect to see intellectual decline and neurological defects becoming prominent soon. These may involve motor, speech or visual function. Myoclonic jerks are almost invariably seen. Cerebellar, parietal or motor symptoms may all occur, as may dysphasia, dysarthria or seizures. Hallucinations or delusions may be marked. In vCJD cortical blindness occurs in a third of cases.

- I would discuss the patient's outcome frankly but sensitively with his family, for CJD most patients die within two years; however, in vCJD death occurs at a median duration of four months (Will *et al.* 1996). After death, I would request a post-mortem to confirm the diagnosis.

Pointers/Pitfalls

- It was feared that vCJD could reach epidemic proportions and a multitude of safeguards have been introduced. These are both systemic, in the production of the carrying vector, and in monitoring and tertiary prevention. The role of psychiatrists in this is identifying cases, and informing the relevant statutory bodies as well as the surgeons, who need to ensure that there was no risk of instrumental contamination.

- Reference:

  Will *et al.* 1996. A new variant of Creutzfeldt–Jacob disease in the UK. *Lancet*, 347, 921–5.

Scenario 21

A 17-year-old girl is brought to the open access clinic by her anxious mother who states that her behaviour has deteriorated and that she is doing poorly at school. They are committed members of an evangelical group and she is concerned that her daughter is no longer 'speaking in tongues' at church. How would you proceed?

Suggested Answers

- Whilst it is important to obtain a comprehensive history and mental state, engaging the client and promoting trust are likely to be important in this case. After observing the interaction between the mother and daughter I would ask the mother to wait outside, and then speak with the patient/daughter.

Scenario 21 *continues*

The patient indicates that she is bored at home, and with her parents' religiosity. Her friends go out to night clubs and she isn't allowed to. It really annoys her. She states that she is doing fine at school, but as she can't join in with her friends they are leaving her behind. What are your thoughts?

Suggested Answers

- I would want to explore this more, to find out whether this is teenage rebelliousness, or intergenerational culture conflict.

- I would look carefully for any symptoms of depression, disorders of thought, possession, stream, or content.

- I would need to determine whether there is any drug use or abuse of any sort going on.

Scenario 21 *continues*

The girl denies any problems. How do you proceed?

Suggested Answers

- Having talked to the daughter, I would ask to speak to the mother alone.

- In particular, I would ask for specific details about the problems at school.

- Also, I would ask her to clarify the deterioration in her daughter's behaviour that she referred to at the initial meeting.

- I would ask what her suspicions are, and whether they relate to drug use.

Scenario 21 *continues*

The mother says that her daughter's grades are slowly slipping, and that she has lost interest in the team sports she used to play. They have wondered about drugs but all she does is sit at home and do nothing. What are the possibilities?

Suggested Answers

- Given this information, I would say that the possibilities include:
  - Depression.
  - Simple schizophrenia.
  - Substance misuse for example, contributing to cannabis causing apathy.
  - No mental illness.

Pointers/Pitfalls

- Simple schizophrenia is characterised by the negative symptoms of schizophrenia with an insidious but progressive onset. It is not preceded by any positive symptoms. There is increasing social impoverishment, idleness and aimlessness.

- Glossolalia, or 'speaking in tongues', is a religiously appropriate act in certain Christian denominations. However, it occurs in sanctioned and controlled occasions, during a service. It is where this is breached that it can be a psychotic phenomenon. Usually the priest or congregants will recognise this abnormality and contact services.

- Reference:

  Littlewood, R., Lipsedge, M. 1997. *Aliens and Alienists: Ethnic Minorities and Psychiatry*. London: Routledge.

Scenario 22

A 22-year-old married male solicitor with no past psychiatric history presents to your clinic with 'panic'. This began shortly after he visited a male brothel whilst on a stag weekend in Amsterdam. How do you proceed?

Suggested Answers

- I would elicit a full history, including the details and circumstances of the visit, and perform a mental state examination.

- In particular I would be interested in the 'panic'. It would be important to clarify whether his symptoms are related to the event or to an independent mental illness.

- I would ask whether the patient experienced the relevant features of fear (paroxysmal or generalised); namely, signs of adrenal stimulation, tachycardia, tachypnoea, sweating, butterflies and nausea.

- Also, I would ask whether there were symptoms of hyperventilation; namely, shortness of breath or tightness in the chest, paraesthesia, or carpo-pedal spasm.

- I would find out if there was any trigger or anticipatory anxiety.

- If there were no abnormalities detected but a marked variant of normal anxiety, then I would suspect that this may be related to an understandable fear of ridicule or exposure.

- I would then advise him to consider counselling, or give him contact numbers for an appropriate group as being reasonable in helping him with his adjustment to his sexuality or the event.

Scenario 22 *continues*

Further questioning reveals that he is convinced that everyone knows he is gay. He is sure because at a team building weekend a colleague who he was sharing a room with kept on bumping into him. What are the possibilities?

Suggested Answers

I would group the possibilities into three groups:

- Neurotic disorders:
  - This might present as severe anxiety precipitated by a previously unusual act, carried out in an environment where inhibitions were lowered by a permissive environment, alcohol, drugs, or a combination of these things. Sexologists have postulated that sexual identity from homosexuality to heterosexuality is a continuum with a cut-off of act performance depending on environmental and developmental factors.
  - The patient may have an AIDS phobia, following protected or unprotected intercourse. If the patient has had unprotected intercourse, then I think it would be important for me to arrange counselling before testing for HIV.
  - I would also consider whether this patient has a coincidental panic disorder.

- Psychotic disorders:
  - I would have to consider whether the patient is suffering from acute and transient psychotic disorder, precipitated by the stress of this event.
  - Alternatively, he may have a delusional disorder.
  - I should also be aware that the patient may be in the early stages of paranoid schizophrenia, which predated the incident or was precipitated by the stress of it, and to which he was vulnerable due to a genetic predisposition.

- Finally, I would look for evidence of an organic disorder, which whilst unusual in this age group, would include those mimicking anxiety disorders
  - Hyperthyroidism.
  - Adrenal tumour.

Pointers/Pitfalls

- In this case it is important not to assume that the patient wishes to be a practising homosexual, but that he may well need help coming to terms with the implications of his actions. If unaware of local facilities the candidate should provide contact details for the local genito-urinary clinic or HIV service, which would be aware of non-statutory organisations able to provide support. The Terrance Higgins Trust is a good start.

- It would also be important to test the fixity of the ideas to ensure that a delusion is not prematurely identified.

Scenario 23

A young female has been taken to A&E on a Saturday night. She was presented by the Police having been found mute and motionless. She had dialled 999 and the Police had traced the call to the phone booth where the patient was still standing. How would you assess her and what is your differential diagnosis?

Suggested Answers

- I would start by attempting to obtain a full history, performing a mental state examination and obtaining relevant collateral information.

- In this case with a mute patient it would be important to speak to the Police Officers who brought her to hospital.

- In particular, I would ask them whether she has been mute all the time, or if it is elective/partial. I would ask if she has responded in any way, if there was an accident, and whether there are any other witnesses.

- I would talk to the nursing staff, who would likewise provide useful observations.

- I would look to see whether the patient is carrying any identifying information such as a wallet or a medical alert bracelet.

- If available, I would use the patient's personal details to contact their next of kin or friends to obtain further details; alternatively, I would search relevant databases such as medical, psychiatric, social, or forensic.

- When assessing the patient directly, I would pay special attention to their appearance and behaviour.

- In particular, I would note whether they were dishevelled, unwashed and odorous, or clean and kempt.

- I would note their style of clothing and its appropriateness for the weather.

- I would determine if the patient is malnourished or dehydrated.

Scenario 23 *continues*

The patient is dressed in a tank-top, black jeans, boots and small earrings. It is midsummer. You note constricted pupils and she is slowly raising her level of consciousness. She has a coloured stamp on her hand. How do you proceed?

Suggested Answers

- I would assess the patient's level of consciousness; in particular, I would note:

  - If the patient is aware of her surroundings, and if her eyes are open (and following events/objects) or closed (responding to stimulation or resisting passive opening).

  - If she responds to stimuli, whether internal or external.

  - Her facial expression – is it sad or perplexed?

- I would assess the patient's posture; in particular, I would note:

  - Whether she looked comfortable or awkward.

  - Whether her posture is maintained regardless of what is said to her, or does it alter.

  - If the patient maintains an awkward posture, does she return to it if repositioned?

- I would consider if she is responding to hallucinations.

- I would be very cautious of inconsistent, exaggerated or paradoxical symptoms.

- I would need to make a full physical and neurological examination.

- In order to do this, I would carefully explain to the patient what I was about to do at each stage.

- In particular, I would carry out the following:

  - I would determine her level of consciousness using the Glasgow Coma Scale.

  - I would examine her for any signs of a delirium or a substance-induced condition.

○ I would look carefully for needle tracks, abscesses, lymphadenopathy, fetor, pupil size; raised intracranial pressure and space-occupying lesions, such as papilloedema, nystagmus, proprioceptive abnormalities and incontinence.

● I would conclude that the patient has probably been to a club and ingested an illicit drug. Nevertheless it would still be advisable to obtain a full blood count (FBC), urea and electrolytes (U&E's), tests of renal and hepatic function and a urine sample, for dipstick testing for metabolites of substances of abuse.

● I would make a note that an MRI or EEG may later prove necessary.

● Other factors that I would like to explore include whether there was any evidence of stressful events in her life and I would be alert to dissociative symptoms and secondary gain. Also I would look out for any social stressors to be avoided, such as domestic violence or criminal charges.

Use this page to write notes

Scenario 23 *continues*

What are the differential diagnoses?

Suggested Answers

My differential diagnoses include:

- Functional
  - Psychogenic
    - Dissociative stupor
    - Factitious disorder – simulation for unconscious gain
  - Non-psychogenic
    - Affective disorders

      Severe depression with/without psychotic symptoms

      Mixed affective state (manic stupor)
    - Catatonic schizophrenia.

- Organic
  - Vascular: cerebrovascular accident (CVA), transient ischaemic attack (TIA)
  - Infective
  - Trauma: head injury
  - Autoimmune
  - Metabolic/endocrine: hypoglycaemia
  - Poisoning: deliberate or accidental
    - Overdose with lithium, neuroleptics, opiates
    - Drugs of misuse, benzodiazepines, 'XTC' (3,4-methylenedioxymetamphetamine), gammahydroxybutyrate (GBH), ketamine.

- Neurological:
  - epilepsy
  - tumour
  - hydrocephalus

- No formal mental illness
  - Malingering (conscious simulation) to avoid:
    - an unpleasant situation (Z76.5)
    - a criminal matter (Z65.0)
    - domestic violence (Z63.0)
    - consequences of a pregnancy (Z64.0).

Pointers/Pitfalls

- In questions involving street drugs candidates need to be aware of changing local fashions. Which drugs are the current ones of choice? Has strength recently altered?

- Cannabis as a leaf used to be about 3–4% delta-tetra-hydro-cannabinol. Resin was slightly stronger. Developments in cultivar selection have produced variants with a dry weight concentration of 15%+ active ingredient. This, predictably, markedly increases the risk of a psychotic reaction, and prolongs duration of action.

- With other illicit drugs purity of product and contamination issues are more relevant.

- The differential listed is deliberately expansive to cover many options which would be eliminated or rendered less likely by the presence of the constricted pupils.

Scenario 24

A 39-year-old female is referred by A&E with rigidity, muscular weakness and falls. There is a four-year history of delusions and auditory hallucinations. Five weeks ago her medication was changed to an atypical antipsychotic, after a relapse with a manic episode. She had been an inpatient for eight weeks. Bipolar affective disorder was diagnosed. What do you do?

Suggested Answers

- I would obtain as much further history as was possible, such as hospital notes, whether hard copies or from an IT source such as remote access archives.

- I would perform a complete physical examination, and investigations are required.

- In particular I would be looking for neurological abnormalities indicating a cerebrovascular event, or a pyrexia and autonomic instability which might indicate neuroleptic malignant syndrome.

- I would also look for any markers of an epileptiform event, such as loss of consciousness, soiling, or aura.

- I would determine whether there was a delirium.

Scenario 24 *continues*

Physical examination reveals bilateral up-going plantars and hyper-reflexia without other sensory impairment or bowel/bladder dysfunction. Fundoscopy reveals bilateral optic atrophy. How do you proceed?

Suggested Answers

- I would want the patient to have an MRI and lumber puncture. The former is needed, as white matter lesions rather than a cerebrovascular event are likely. The latter would be for CSF analysis.

- If white matter lesions are confirmed then I would refer the patient to neurology, or another appropriate specialty.

- I would consider prescribing steroids for the patient if her condition is established to have a neurological cause with an autoimmune basis.

- In either case, I would plan to review her prognosis and treatment, as well as her long-term care plans depending upon the prognosis for her future self-care.

- I would liaise with Social Services and request carer assessments, as they may be useful.

Scenario 24 *continues*

Oligoclonal bands are found. MRI reveals bilateral periventricular high-signal areas, also seen in both hemispheres and brainstem. A diagnosis of multiple sclerosis is made. Her antipsychotic is stopped and treatment with steroids begun. Is there any association between lesions and psychotic symptoms in multiple sclerosis?

Suggested Answers

- Yes; more lesions in total and more in the temporal horns. However, florid psychosis is rare, occurring in less than 5% of cases.

Pointers/Pitfalls

- Reference: Feinstein *et al*. 1992. Psychotic illness in multiple sclerosis. A clinical and magnetic resonance imaging study. *British Journal of Psychiatry*, 161, 680–5.

Scenario 25

You are asked to see a 45-year-old male who states that he wishes to have the lower part of his leg amputated. What do you do?

Suggested Answers

- I consider it vital to take a comprehensive history from this patient, and obtain collateral information where possible.

- I would need to determine whether he is depressed and suffering from an affect congruent delusion, particularly a nihilistic one, or whether he has a 'bizarre' delusion indicating a schizophreniform process.

- I would find out whether he has command hallucinations to cast off the offending body part, or if he suffers from passivity phenomena.

- I would investigate whether there is substance misuse.

- I would find out whether the patient has illness beliefs relating to his or his family's illnesses, such as a history of cancer in the lower limb.

- I would determine whether he has a physical condition such as diabetes or neuropathic pain.

- I would find out about his support networks and current stressors, and if he has been in an accident and, if so, if there is litigation.

- I think it essential to consult his GP and get his past medical records.

Scenario 25 *continues*

You discover that there is no affective or schizophreniform disorder. The patient has felt since the age of ten that his lower leg was not part of his body. Whilst he is not depressed it does make him unhappy. How do you proceed?

Suggested Answers

- In this case I would proceed firstly by classifying his disorder, which, in ICD-10 terms, is a hypochondriacal disorder. In DSM-IV the patient has body dysmorphic disorder.

- I would be aware that if the beliefs are of delusional intensity then there would also be a delusional disorder.

- I would consider which medications would be helpful. In particular, I would realise that antipsychotics are not particularly effective. I may consider prescribing SSRI's, which have been used with some success in treating body dysmorphic disorder.

- If there are any secondary conditions such as social anxiety disorder, obsessive compulsive disorder, or a personality disorder, I would treat them as appropriate.

- I would consider referring the patient for psychotherapy, as this can also be of assistance.

- There is a morbidity associated with unsuccessful treatment, and so I would monitor the patient for the development of maladaptive coping mechanisms or a depression.

Scenario 25 *continues*

After 18 months of treatment, during which you have spoken with an expert in body dysmorphic disorder, there is little change and the patient demands surgery to remove the limb. What do you do?

Suggested Answers

- Assuming that the patient has engaged with treatment, I would think it likely that medication and therapy have little more to offer. I would classify the questions around surgery as being of capacity and service provision. Providing that the patient understands the consequences of his actions, then I would consider him likely to have capacity. I would ask for a second opinion from another psychiatrist, consult my defence organisation and refer him to a surgeon before recommending surgery for amputation.

- I understand the issues around service provision to be more focused on the legality of amputating a healthy limb and finding a surgeon prepared to undertake the operation rather than on cost. I understand that removing a healthy limb may be an offence of 'maim' and that a defence of battery may not withstand the assertion that consent was obtained.

- I would be aware that in 1993 the House of Lords considered a case of consenting sado-masochistic practices including branding and genital surgery.

- In particular, the subsequent Law Commission report recommended that 'the intentional causing of serious disabling injury to another person should continue to be criminal, even if the person injured consents to such injury or to the risk of such injury'. Whilst an exception to this was made for proper medical treatment, including gender reassignment, I would be aware that amputation for body dysmorphic disorder was not mentioned. So I would not be sure of the legality of this course of treatment and would proceed extremely cautiously.

Pointers/Pitfalls

- Be aware of when to ask colleagues and outside experts, as well as making sure that the examiner understands you are aware.

- Note that small changes in risk profile may change the unacceptable to the desirable and lawful. For example, were the patient considering auto-amputation, then a harm reduction approach through surgical intervention may well place amputation into the realm of 'proper medical treatment' rather than that of a criminal act.

- Whilst this is a difficult question the principles dealt with have featured in the national press in recent years.

- References:

  Veal, D. 2001. Cognitive behavioural disorder for body dysmorphic disorder. *Advances in Psychiatric Treatment*, 7, 125–32.

  Regina vs Brown [1993] 2 All ER 75.

  Skegg, P.D.G. 1984. *Law Ethics and Medicine*. Oxford: Clarendon, p. 38.

Scenario 26

An 18-year-old male has been referred to you by his GP as he is 'uncomfortable with his sexuality'. How would you proceed?

Suggested Answers

- As this referral is extremely vague and lacking in detail, I would first seek further information.

- I would assume that the 'uncomfortable with his sexuality' refers to the patient and ascertain whether there was a primary care liaison nurse (PCLN). If there was, they would be the first person I would go to for further information, as they could clarify whether the patient had homosexual feelings or if there were other issues. If there was no PCLN, I would advise the patient to attend counselling through a local organisation or self-help group and give him the appropriate contact numbers. I would arrange a session with a PCLN, as this may be useful.

- If I discovered that the issue was a paraphilia that was causing psychological distress, either primary or secondary to interference with social function, then I think it would be proper to refer the patient to a specialist psycho-sexual clinic.

- If it was another issue, then I would arrange for an assessment with a doctor; in particular, it would be important to determine if there was a mental illness or not.

- Aware that the patient may have a lot invested in their first meeting, I would warn them that the assessment would be detailed and may be on-going.

Scenario 26 *continues*

The patient states that his genitalia are repugnant. How do you proceed?

Suggested Answers

- I would need to clarify what the patient means by this statement.

- In particular, I would need to determine whether this feeling is secondary to a psychotic process such as a delusion, a somatic phenomenon such as 'succubus', ie a tactile hallucination of genital engulfment that is associated with self-mutilation. Alternatively, it might be secondary to organic dysfunction such as deformity (hypo/epispadia), injury or hermaphrodism. Finally, it might be a culture-bound syndrome akin to Koro or an overvalued idea.

Scenario 26 *continues*

Further exploration reveals that the patient has known that they were born the wrong sex from the age of seven. He is more comfortable in female clothing and wears it at weekends and on holiday. How do you proceed?

Suggested Answers

- I think it would be important to interview informants to obtain a full background to this case.

- In particular, I would find it useful to have pictures of the patient, as they provide evidence of living as a different sex, the adjustments made, and are an indicator of the steps taken by the patient.

- My assessment would include looking for any evidence of obstetric or developmental abnormalities; for example, prenatal or perinatal illnesses or operations; exposure to feminising hormones; and developmental milestones.

- In my discussions with the patient, I would try to find out the following information:
  - When they first cross-dressed.
  - When they first knew that they were the wrong sex.
  - The patient's ideas on gender identity and roles; a sound knowledge of this is important.
  - Whether they enjoy the cross-dressing and, if so, why.
  - In particular, I would ask them if cross-dressing makes them feel comfortable and look good, or feel sexually aroused, which would indicate paraphilia or transvestism.
  - To clarify the difference between his sexual identity and gender, I would ask the patient if he fantasises about men or women.

- I would ask the patient what he wishes to achieve, and whether he wants advice, hormone treatment or surgery. In addition, I would want to make a formal assessment of the patient's personality.

- In particular, I would want to know about his intelligence, coping mechanisms and social adjustment.

- Other areas that I would concentrate on are whether the patient is responding to stresses in his life, or if he has a deeply ingrained pattern of cognition, affect or behaviour developed through the parenting style he experienced or other life events.

- It would be important for me to assess the social adjustments that the patient has made in their life. In particular, I would ask whether his friends and colleagues know and how he relates to members of either sex. I would clarify the level of explanation he has given for his cross-dressing or sexuality, as well as find out what social consequences to cross-dressing he has experienced and how he coped with them.

- If the patient expressed an interest in continuing, then I would outline my proposed management.

- In particular, I would need to appraise the patient that the process was a life-long commitment, and at some stage would be irreversible. I would need to be satisfied that he had not underestimated the physical and social risks, or overestimated the benefits of a sex-change operation to his quality of life.

- I would then explain the stages of gender reassignment.

- I would explain that in the first stage the patient would concentrate on social modification.

  ○ In particular, I would explain how the patient would need to dress and behave like a woman all the time for an appropriate period.

  ○ I would be aware that they may require assistance with dressing, make-up and hair removal.

  ○ I would explain that the patient would need to learn different styles of conversation, comportment and body posture/gestures.

- I would explain that if this was a success then oestrogen treatment would be appropriate. I would make the patient aware that there were risks and side-effects.

  ○ These include acne, thrombosis and an increased risk of breast cancer.

207

○ Weepiness and lability of mood, although this is not always unwelcome as it may appear congruent with feminisation.

● After a year of this, if there was good social adjustment and no other condition emerged, and the patient wished to continue, then I would advise the patient that a sex change operation would be appropriate.

Pointers/Pitfalls

Transsexualism (F64.0) has three criteria:

1. The desire to live and be accepted as a member of the opposite sex, usually accompanied by the wish to make his or her body as congruent as possible with the preferred sex through surgery and hormone treatment.

2. The transsexual identity has been present persistently for at least two years.

3. The disorder is not a symptom of another mental disorder or a chromosomal abnormality.

Dual-role transvestism (F64.1) has three criteria:

1. The individual wears clothes of the opposite sex in order to experience temporary membership in the opposite sex.

2. There is no sexual motivation for the cross-dressing.

3. The individual has no desire for a permanent change to the opposite sex.

- At the opening of parliament in the Winter of 2003 Her Majesty's Government declared its wish to introduce a Gender Recognition Bill (2003). This would bring British legislation into line with its European Union obligations.

- The legislation brings into place a process whereby individuals who have already received gender realignment may be fast tracked to receive 'official' recognition of their new sex with all its attendant rights. All new applicants would require scrutiny by approved individuals which would be consultants at gender reassignment clinics and certain legal members.

- One obligation in the legislation is that reassignees must inform prospective marriage partners of their status for the marriage to be recognisable.

209

- There remains debate over the length of time that potential reassignees must live as their preferred gender, but at least a year is recommended before beginning any irreversible steps.

- Reference:

Roberts, J. 2004. Escape from normality. *BMJ* 328: 962.

Scenario 27

You are an SHO working in a child and adolescent mental health services (CAMHS) clinic. You are referred an eight-year-old boy who has been overly active since a baby, by his GP. His school is concerned that his academic work is seriously impaired by his difficulty in concentrating. How do you proceed?

Suggested Answers

- Whilst there are several diagnostic possibilities I would be aware that attention deficit hyperactivity disorder (ADHD) must be considered as a possible diagnosis.

- I would obtain a school report having obtained parental consent.

- A full history and examination of the child is essential as is meeting all the members of the household. In the history I would pay particular attention to any symptoms of poor concentration, overactivity and impulsivity. I would ask if these symptoms occur at home, and school.

- Other important areas are family history and if there any concurrent medical conditions.

- I would also seek evidence of any attachment difficulties or anxiety.

- On the basis of my findings I may request the completion of Connor's rating scales at school and home.

Scenario 27 *continues*

You find that Connor's scores are significantly increased, and history and examination are compatible with a diagnosis of ADHD. How do you proceed?

Suggested Answers

- I would discuss with the parents the nature, prognosis and treatment of ADHD.

- Specifically, I would ask their consent to give the diagnosis to the school so the boy's special educational needs could be better met.

- Psychoeducation would include the use of appropriate parental strategies to encourage better concentration, eg gaining eye contact first before giving the child an order, and providing a stable and structured home environment. Some parents find a parenting skills course beneficial.

- If these interventions are unsuccessful then I would discuss the use of stimulant medication with the parents.

Scenario 27 *continues*

The psychosocial interventions you suggested are unsuccessful. Outline your medical management.

Suggested Answers

- I would take baseline height and weight measurements of the child, and check for any contraindications to medication.

- I would choose methylphenidate, and begin with a dose of 5 mg bd after meals.

- I would warn the parents of possible side-effects, including anorexia, poor sleep, tearfulness or sadness, suspiciousness and facial tics.

- If low-dose treatment is acceptable I would titrate the dose of medication until a satisfactory response is obtained.

Scenario 27 *continues*

Treatment with methylphenidate is unsuccessful due to anorexia and mood disturbance. What other drug choices are available? Are there any precautions you may need to take in using these?

Suggested Answers

- Other options would include dexamphetamine, imipramine, clonidine and risperidone.

- I would seek the advice of my Consultant in using these, and discuss with them if I should use the pharmacy drug information line for advice.

- Licences are not granted for most of these drugs in children, and I would advise the parents of this.

- Regarding imipramine I would perform an ECG before prescribing, as well as undertaking a cardiovascular examination.

Pointers/Pitfalls

- In child and adolescent psychiatry, in addition to stating the obvious of obtaining a history and performing an examination, it is nearly always practical to state that you would gain background reports, eg from school.

- In addition, always say that you would meet the whole family or members of the household when assessing a young person: context is very important for children.

- Mentioning the most obvious diagnosis at the start is a good strategy as it alerts the examiners to your appropriate thinking. It is important though to be seen as being flexible and that your mind is not made up in any direction.

- The model answer sets high standards in terms of relevance, conciseness and applying specialist knowledge. Don't panic if you do not know all of it! The examiners will want to see you demonstrate that overactivity does not necessarily mean ADHD, and that a diagnosis of ADHD does not necessarily mean immediate drug treatment.

- Don't be frightened to admit your ignorance and say that you don't know, eg to the last stem: many candidates will not have this knowledge. Those who do will score very highly, and if you have answered reasonably well to this point you should pass comfortably. Often examiners will probe more deeply to try to give a candidate more marks – a difficult question may be a good sign!

- Don't be afraid to say that you would use resources, such as your Consultant, the BNF or whatever seems appropriate.

Scenario 28

You are an SpR working in child and adolescent psychiatry. You have received a referral from the paediatric SHO about a 14-year-old young woman who has been admitted for unexplained weight loss. The SHO explains that no physical cause has been found and that the patient has been reluctant to eat on the ward. Outline your management.

Suggested Answers

- The differential diagnosis for this case includes an eating disorder (such as an anorexia nervosa) and a mood disorder.

- To confirm that the situation was not an emergency I would wish to ask the SHO for her weight, BMI (body mass index) and current hydration status.

- To establish the diagnosis I would take a history from, and perform a mental state examination of, the patient, as well as meet her family.

- Reading her medical notes will also be useful, and I would discuss her behaviour on the ward with a senior nurse.

- Telephoning her school for information with parental consent would also be useful.

Scenario 28 *continues*

Your history reveals that the patient has been limiting her calorie intake for over one year. There are no clear features of a mood disorder. What information from the history will be particularly relevant to check for an eating disorder?

Suggested Answers

- I would enquire about the following: cessation of periods, self-induced vomiting, increased exercise, use of laxatives, disordered body image.

Scenario 28 *continues*

You establish a diagnosis of anorexia nervosa. Outline your initial management.

Suggested Answers

- I would discuss with the paediatric team their current plan for the patient. If the patient's physical condition is stable and her BMI is within acceptable limits then outpatient treatment is likely to be the preferred option. If not, then remaining on the paediatric unit or transfer to a specialist in-patient eating disorders unit for adolescents should be considered.

Scenario 28 *continues*

The patient's condition allows an outpatient treatment programme.
What will this consist of?

Suggested Answers

- This is dependent on discussion with the family and young person and her current condition, but I would consider including family therapy, individual work with the patient (such as CBT), psychoeducation and monitoring of weight.

- If her weight falls significantly, I would reconsider admission.

- I would also monitor the patient's mood and determine if there are any acts or ideas of deliberate self-harm.

- The programme requires a multidisciplinary approach, and as well as possible family therapist and clinical psychologist involvement, I consider a referral to a dietician is indicated. In some areas a specialist team may be able to undertake the work.

Scenario 28 *continues*

Despite an outpatient treatment programme the patient's BMI is now 13, and the decision is made that she requires urgent admission to hospital, but she refuses. How do you proceed?

Suggested Answers

- I would gain the parents' opinion. If they are in agreement with the admission then I would use either the Mental Health Act or The Children Act to effect admission.

- If the parents are not in agreement then I would ask for Social Services' opinion as a matter of urgency as to whether her parents' wishes should be overridden.

Pointers/Pitfalls

- At several points in this model answer emergency management is discussed, even when this is not asked for specifically by the examiner. If you can show to the examiners that you are thinking safety, safety, safety, then you will be well on the way to passing.

- If you can show an ability to prioritise information, eg 'What is the patient's BMI? Is she dehydrated?' then the examiners will see you as a thoughtful, proactive and, above all, safe candidate who should pass.

- You do not have to go into precise figures for the BMI to show competency: understanding of process here is more important. Similarly, it is Social Services' responsibility to consider further action, so you do not need to say that she may be made a Ward of Court, although if you have this information then you could add it.

- Don't forget the multidisciplinary team, which is very important in CAMHS work. This also show the examiners that you are not a one-person band, and can work with other people in an integrated and thorough way.

Scenario 29

You are SHO working in a CAMHS clinic. An educational welfare officer (EWO) refers you a 15-year-old young woman who has not attended school for one academic term. Outline your management.

Suggested Answers

- I would attempt to gain as much information as possible from the EWO, and ask if there is any possible reason identified for this patient's school refusal. A formal school report would also be helpful.

- I would then meet the patient, her parents, probably the rest of her family, and if appropriate the EWO.

- A history and mental state examination may reveal a cause for her school non-attendance.

Scenario 29 *continues*

You gain a history of lowered mood for approximately one year associated with some biological features of depression. What further
information do you require?

Suggested Answers

- I would wish to know if the patient has acted on or had any ideas of deliberate self-harm, and establish by examination if there is any evidence of psychosis.

- Having done this, I would begin to look for any precipitants and maintaining factors of the depression. It may be necessary to interview the patient alone to obtain some of this information.

Scenario 29 *continues*

From your history it appears that the lowered mood began when her step-father moved in. She appears to be angry towards him but does not express her feelings. What goes through your mind over why this may be the case?

Suggested Answers

- I would wonder if she is being hurt in any way by her step-father. Less seriously, she may have had some of her mother's attention taken away from her and she is jealous of her step-father.

- More concerning are the hypotheses that her step-father is abusing her physically or sexually. However, other possibilities do exist.

Scenario 29 *continues*

Alone, the patient reveals to you that her step-father is having consenting sex with her. How do you proceed?

Suggested Answers

- The patient is being sexually abused. I would terminate the interview at this point to avoid the contamination of information, ensure that she does not have immediate contact with her step-father, find a member of staff to sit with her, and telephone Social Services immediately to ask their advice as how to proceed.

Pointers/Pitfalls

- School refusal is a description of behaviour. It is not a diagnosis.

- The EWO is likely to have a lot of useful information, and may be a good person to invite to a first meeting to help engage with the family.

- It helps to show that you are safe if you highlight looking for suicidal ideas and psychosis in depression.

- Don't go down the route of stating that you would prescribe an anti-depressant for her without thinking about why the patient is sad!

- It is a common mistake to contaminate evidence by continuing an interview after a disclosure has been made. If you discuss the abuse with the victim, in Court it may be alleged that you gave her ideas around which she fabricated a story. Once you have tele-phoned Social Services it is their responsibility to advise you how to proceed.

Scenario 30

You are an SpR working in a paediatric liaison service. You are referred a 13-year-old male who is persistently tired, sleeps excessively and has reduced activity. As there has been no physical diagnosis made, the paediatric consultant has asked you to undertake an assessment of what appears to be chronic fatigue syndrome. How do you proceed?

Suggested Answers

- Chronic fatigue syndrome is often a challenging condition to treat. I would obtain information from the Consultant and the medical notes, especially about the family's attitude to the symptoms.

- In particular, are they open to the possibility of there being a psychological component to the illness, and are they aware of the psychiatric referral?

- Having done so, I would obtain a history and mental state examination of the patient, and meet the family.

Scenario 30 *continues*

Your assessment confirms a diagnosis of chronic fatigue syndrome and no severe mental illness. What treatment can be offered?

Suggested Answers

- The treatment options that I would offer include: psychoeducation, a behavioural programme of increased activity, individual CBT and family meetings.

Scenario 30 *continues*

The parents are reluctant that their son be forced to increase his activity, as they are convinced that he has an undiagnosed physical illness, and activity may physically damage him. How do you proceed?

Suggested Answers

- I would explore the reasons for the parents' beliefs. It may be helpful to consider their own past medical and past psychiatric histories, as well as discussing with them what has happened previously to their son when he has exercised more.

- I would also wish to determine what secondary gain there is for the patient through his behaviour, and to consider what effect or gain it might bring to the family functioning.

Scenario 30 *continues*

The parents are reluctant to engage in discussing themselves or the family with you, and instead are intending to visit different alternative medicine practitioners. They seem angry at your line of questioning. What would you do now?

Suggested Answers

- I would acknowledge their emotions and ask them why they are angry. It may be appropriate to let the parents know that my involvement will still be open to them if they wish to reconsider there being some psychological basis to their son's symptoms.

- Some authorities in this case suggest an approach of letting parents exhaust their quest for physical cure and treatment so that they can become engaged with psychological treatment options. In some cases, especially if a child is not attending school, referral to Social Services is indicated to promote the child's welfare.

Pointers/Pitfalls

- Engagement and working together with parents is often a challenge in these cases. If you know this then emphasise it up front.

- It is good to state the obvious, eg read the medical notes.

- In the last answer the third person is adopted, which is a useful style for emphasising the tentative nature of the response.

- Overall, this question would be demanding for nearly all candidates, and examiners would be aware of that. Child questions often cause examinees considerable anxiety, especially if they have not done a child job. In an example such as this one, however, there are many appropriate strategies from adult liaison that could be used, eg acknowledge to the patient that their fatigue is real to them, explore underlying illness beliefs, etc.

- However, if you are stuck by a question then don't, whatever you do, pretend that you know the answer – the examiners are likely to see through your pretence quickly! In this case, for example, you can say that you would discuss the case with your Consultant for further advice, once you had outlined some basic management.

251

Scenario 31

You are a Consultant general adult psychiatrist on-call. You are awoken by a call from a GP at the local airport who reports that a middle-aged man has barricaded himself into a room in the airport, claims he has a knife and states that he will kill himself if approached, because the 'voices' have told him to. How do you proceed?

Suggested Answers

- This is an emergency situation that requires careful management to minimise the risk posed by this man to himself and others. I would check that the Police have been called and are in attendance. It would also be important for the GP to obtain any details about this man's family in order to request their attendance and to provide background information. I would attend the scene straight away.

Scenario 31 *continues*

When you arrive at the airport you are told by the Police that an unknown man has recently arrived from a flight from Ghana, and has barricaded himself into a toilet. Initial negotiations have begun, but it is difficult to understand him. How do you proceed?

Suggested Answers

- I would ask the Police what their current assessment of the man's dangerousness is, and whether he has a weapon.

- I would ask how the negotiations have been carried out and how the Police have ensured their own safety. As Police Officers have some experience of mental illness, I would ask about their impression of the man's mental state.

- In addition, I would find out whether the Ghanaian High Commission has been contacted for any leads on the man's identity. If he is a Ghanaian national, I would ask if they could provide a member of staff to be involved in giving advice in the negotiations.

Scenario 31 *continues*

The Police Officer in charge explains to you that it is unclear if the man has a weapon, and so his risk is uncertain, but the Police have been able to conduct negotiations at a distance by raising their voice from around a corner. Their impression is that the man has a mental illness. High Commission staff are on their way. The Police offer you a safe telephone link with the man to conduct a limited interview. What do you ask him?

Suggested Answers

- I would give him an opportunity to speak and discuss what his current concerns are, having introduced myself and my role.

- I would also undertake a brief mental state examination, looking particularly for evidence of psychosis or major affective disorder. I would hope to form an opinion on his immediate safety, as well as asking him what could be done to help him, if anything.

Scenario 31 *continues*

You discuss the information you have obtained with the Police, and state that the man appears to be psychotic, having delusional beliefs that he is being pursued by terrorists associated with third person auditory hallucinations. He believes that he would be better killing himself with the knife he has rather than letting them murder him. He does not wish any help, other than being left alone. The Police ask you for advice about how to proceed, and point out that they have not yet been able to negotiate him out.

Suggested Answers

- I would advise the Police to keep talking non-directively to the man as a means to distract him and improve rapport. This is a complicated situation in which the balance of forcible extraction with the risks of precipitating self-harm and violence to others should be weighed against continuing to talk to the man with the risk of him self-harming anyway in the context of an untreated psychotic illness. A decision requires to be taken by the Police on the basis of the advice I supply. Depending on the circumstances, the 1983 Mental Health Act (in England and Wales) would be used. If not already done so, I would ensure that an ambulance was on-site and that there was an appropriately identified intensive care bed available for this man.

Pointers/Pitfalls

- This is the sort of PMP that makes candidates especially nervous, as it is a novel situation where critical decisions require to be taken quickly. However, a lot of the management is common sense: make sure that you and the patient are safe; take a (brief) history and exam; work in collaboration with the Police.

- Don't get into the position of saying whether the toilet should be stormed! The Police are the experts in forcible extraction and not you!

- Starting with the 'This is an emergency situation' gives you some breathing space, and lets the examiners know that you have understood the nature of the scenario.

- Some Consultants might delegate the SpR to attend the airport, but for the exam (and in real life) you would be ill advised to do so!

Scenario 32

You are an SpR working in your outpatient clinic. A GP telephones you, saying that he has come to visit a 25-year-old woman who lives alone who is three weeks post-partum. He is concerned about her as she is mute.

Suggested Answers

- This is an emergency situation. From the description given by the GP this woman may be suffering post-natal depression or post-partum psychosis. The risk of harm to her baby or her is very high. It is vital that she is not left alone until adequately assessed by a psychiatrist. I would advise the GP that he or another health professional should stay with the woman until she is seen.

Scenario 32 *continues*

The GP explains that he cannot stay as he has been called to another emergency. How do you proceed?

Suggested Answers

- I would advise the GP on the risks of this course of action, stating that the patient is at immediate risk. However, I would leave the clinic to attend the patient's house immediately if no other member of staff was available.

Scenario 32 *continues*

You attend the patient's house. After some time you form the opinion, on the little information you obtain, that the woman is suffering from a major depressive disorder. She does not want to go to hospital, saying that she wants her and her baby left alone. How do you proceed?

Suggested Answers

- In view of the immediate risk mother and baby are at I would detain the patient in hospital. To safeguard the baby's welfare I would involve Social Services to ensure that there is an appropriate plan adopted for the baby's care. Ideally this should involve the joint admission of mother and child.

Pointers/Pitfalls

- Think safety all the time here – you can always catch up on your outpatient clinic another time; you can't bring mother and baby back from the dead.

- Don't forget about the baby and their welfare.

Scenario 33

You are the on-call Consultant general adult psychiatrist. In the evening the duty SHO telephones you to inform you that an in-patient has committed suicide by hanging themselves on the ward. How do you proceed?

Suggested Answers

- This is a distressing situation for the patient's family, as well as the ward staff. However, I would first establish that appropriate attempts had been made to resuscitate the patient. In particular, I would ask whether the patient has been taken to the local A&E Department, whether an ambulance has been called and if basic CPR was undertaken on the ward. Assuming these steps had been undertaken I would attend the ward.

- When there, I would discuss the situation with the nurse-in-charge of the ward, the SHO and the duty manager or nurse-in-charge of the hospital. If there is a serious incident policy I would ask for a copy of this. Several areas require planning: informing the next-of-kin, ensuring the continuing safety of patients on the ward, informing the Police, and in due course alerting the Coroner or Procurator Fiscal. The ward staff are likely to need support at this time, and as the duty Consultant I would see this as part of my responsibility. I would also consider informing the patient's RMO (Responsible Medical Officer), even if they are not on duty. The following day senior management should be contacted, who will inform the Press Officer of developments.

Scenario 33 *continues*

The patient is certified dead, and your advice is carried through. As part of the investigations afterwards you notice that there have been several serious incidents on the ward, each of which has involved patients under the care of the same RMO. How do you proceed?

Suggested Answers

- This is a difficult situation, but as a doctor I have a responsibility to the public that they receive good care from my professional colleagues. It may be that, as part of the investigation, these concerns have been noted by other members of the investigating committee and discussed by them. If not, then I would raise them in the first instance with the Trust Medical Director to ask for advice as to how to proceed.

Pointers/Pitfalls

- This is an unusual situation, but if you think in a pragmatic way and use common sense then you will do well.

- Never believe that someone is dead until appropriate attempts have been made to resuscitate them.

- As the unfolding scenario is complex, it is appropriate to take advice from the highest medical level of Trust management. In general, though, it is the Medical Director who should be contacted about a professional colleague who may be failing who works in the same Trust, rather than the General Medical Council.

Scenario 34

You are an SHO working in an affective disorders unit. A 35-year-old woman has been referred with a severe depressive illness that has been unresponsive to treatment. How do you proceed?

Suggested Answers

- I would first confirm the diagnosis by taking a history, performing a mental state examination, taking an informant history and reading the patient's past notes. Psychiatric co-morbidity should be excluded, along with physical illness as a cause of the mood disturbance. I would also confirm that the patient has been given and taken a sufficient variety of antidepressants at sufficient dose, each of which has been prescribed over a sufficient period of time. This will confirm or refute a diagnosis of treatment-resistant depression.

Scenario 34 *continues*

You confirm the diagnosis. She has taken fluoxetine, venlafaxine and moclobemide each separately for six weeks. How do you proceed?

Suggested Answers

- Specific advice would depend on the findings from history and examination. However, in general terms, I would ensure that higher doses of the fluoxetine and venlafaxine had been given. If not, then high doses individually of each of these drugs could be used. Augmentation with a mood stabiliser may be suitable. Adding L-tryptophan or thyroxine are also options. If this fails then antidepressant combinations are possible. If there is evidence of psychosis then an antipsychotic should be added. However, the evidence for many of these drug combinations is relatively poor, and I would seek advice from my Consultant in this specialist area, as well as ensuring adequate monitoring of the patient. In addition, some of these combinations have significant safety issues, and will be contraindicated for some, such as the TCA and MAOI combination.

- I would also ensure that any psychosocial precipitants had been addressed as far as possible. Has CBT been attempted? If not, is this because the patient is too depressed to make use of this treatment?

- In severe cases, especially if there is evidence of suicidal ideation or psychosis, admission may be required. Electroconvulsive therapy (ECT) may be considered if further drug treatment is ineffective or emergency treatment is needed. In severe intractable cases psychosurgery may be indicated.

Pointers/Pitfalls

- Treatment-resistant depression can occur in several areas of the exam. The answer given here is very slick – you will not get your words out as smoothly as this when you talk, but don't worry!

- The answer is also very methodical: it starts with the basics, proceeds to using the treatments the patient is currently on, and then discusses treatments of increasing risk. It has a balance between specifics and generalities as well.

- Examiners may have an opportunity to guide you to a specific example from within the more general scenario presented, or may discuss one of the treatments (such as ECT) in more depth.

INDEX